COMPUTER
SECURITY
HANDBOOK

COMPUTER SECURITY HANDBOOK

Strategies and Techniques for Preventing Data Loss or Theft

Rolf T. Moulton

Prentice-Hall, Inc.
Business and Professional Division
Englewood Cliffs, New Jersey

Prentice-Hall International, Inc., London
Prentice-Hall of Australia, Pty. Ltd., *Sydney*
Prentice-Hall Canada, Inc., *Toronto*
Prentice-Hall of India Private Ltd., *New Delhi*
Prentice-Hall of Japan, Inc., *Tokyo*
Prentice-Hall of Southeast Asia Pte. Ltd., *Singapore*
Whitehall Books, Ltd., *Wellington, New Zealand*
Editora Prentice-Hall do Brasil Ltda., *Rio de Janeiro*
Prentice-Hall Hispanoamericana, S.A., *Mexico*

© 1986 *by*
PRENTICE-HALL, INC.
Englewood Cliffs, N.J.

Editor: George E. Parker

Library of Congress Cataloging-in-Publication Data

Moulton, Rolf T.
  Computer security handbook.

  Includes index.
  1. Computers—Access control.   2. Electronic
data processing departments—Security measures.
I. Title.
QA76.9.A25M68   1986   005.8   85-19124

ISBN 0-13-165804-2

Printed in the United States of America

To Diana and Mark;
and to a special friend who was always there.

Acknowledgments

I would like to express my deep appreciation to friends and colleagues in business, government, and academe who helped make this *Handbook* a reality by allowing me to incorporate their work, discuss ideas and concepts, and who provided continuing support and encouragement. Most are unnamed because the list would be too long, but some were so influential that, at the risk of unintentionally offending those who are not mentioned, I must name a few. Permit me to acknowledge Mayor Ed Koch for encouraging the creation of the Computer Security Services Unit and the TOP 40 Program; Commissioners of Investigation Stanley Lupkin and Patrick McGinley, and Dr. Kenneth King for helping convince me that computer security was a good career choice; Deputy Commissioner of Investigation Gordon Haesloop and Detective Frank Nevins for demonstrating and demanding investigative excellence; Bob Courtney, Bob Jacobson, Bill Murray, Donn Parker, Marty Silverman, and Sandy Mann for getting me started in the right direction and continuing to share their extensive knowledge of security and management practices; John O'Mara and Jerry Lobel for both encouraging me to share my security experiences and providing the opportunities to do so; the many Sohioans who made suggestions and cheered me on; Brad Schultz and George Parker for getting the *Handbook* started; and Sybil Grace for producing the *Handbook*.

Author's note: The opinions and recommendations expressed in this *Handbook* are those of Mr. Moulton. They do not represent those of The Standard Oil Company (Ohio) or its subsidiaries.

Contents

CHAPTER 3
Defining Your Computer Security Responsibilities   37

CHAPTER 4
How to Control Computer System Users   59

CHAPTER 9
What to Do When You Are Victimized   151

CHAPTER 10
How to Deal with Disruptions and Disasters   177

Introduction

This *Handbook* was written to help managers make cost-effective decisions about the security measures that are needed to protect their information systems. It presents security fundamentals and practical improvement recommendations for business people, government officials, security officers, data processors, and auditors who are responsible for the protection of computer-related assets such as money and information.

Use this *Handbook* to get the full benefit from your computer security program. That benefit is the reduction of future loss potentials at a cost commensurate with the level of risk that management wishes to assume.

The need for a practical approach to computer security is stressed throughout this *Handbook* because security is primarily a people problem. People, not computers, must design, implement, and maintain controls to prevent other people from diminishing the organization's assets and credibility. People, not computers, must comply with the laws, regulations, policies, and practices that govern how an organization conducts its business affairs.

The people problem issue first became apparent to me in the 1960s when I became personally aware of a successful scheme to prevent the termination of an employee by a management-approved alteration of computerized records. The employee was saved from dismissal because his personnel records, which were used for the preparation of layoff decisions, were modified in a manner that did not affect his payroll records.

The people problem issue continued to be apparent when, years later, I had the direct responsibility for both preventing computer-related fraud and abuse, and dealing with actual computer abuse situations. It had become obvious that people problems could be solved by implementing practical people-oriented security programs that both management and employees would accept.

The *Handbook* is a guide that will give you the understanding of computerized controls necessary to determine if your computer security program is adequate to protect you and your organization from losses and embarrassment. It will show you how to develop an action plan to establish priorities and identify and improve critical controls. It will also help you to deal with computer system realities from a management perspective.

The *Handbook* presents a manager's approach to dealing with security questions such as:

What are my computer security responsibilities?

How do I control what my computer and data are being used for?

How do I prevent errors and omissions?

How do I keep the hackers out of my computer?

Is my computer disaster recovery plan adequate?

How do I keep from getting adverse audit reports?

It also provides guidance for handling special situations that include supervising computer security officers, terminating EDP employees, protecting microcomputers, and collecting computer abuse evidence.

Security is a management responsibility. You, as a manager, must demand that adequate, cost-effective controls be an integral part of your operations. Use the *Handbook* to help you understand and direct the efforts of those people who must work with you to protect the organization's assets. You are the boss. You are the only person who can make the organization's computer security program a reality.

chapter 1
Developing a Practical View of Computer Security

This chapter introduces the subject of computer security. It describes and puts into perspective the security problems that a manager must address, and it provides a proven action plan to start making improvements.

1.1 THE DIFFERENCE BETWEEN INTENTIONAL AND UNINTENTIONAL LOSSES

Every organization must expect some degree of loss to be incurred during the conduct of its operations. The losses may be the result of equipment failures, incorrect staff actions, a natural catastrophe, or dishonest actions by employees or outside individuals.

It would be unreasonable to believe that any organization could prevent all losses. Therefore, the object of every loss prevention program must be to reduce losses to a predefined level of tolerability which is based on the consequences of losses and the costs of preventing those losses.

The extent of losses that can result from the use of a computer can be directly related to the value of the assets that are controlled by the computer and the losses that could result from the misapplication of those assets. An extreme example of a loss that could result from the

1

misapplication of a computer-controlled asset would be the accidental launching of a nuclear missile by its computerized activation system. The consequences of this asset loss would be, at minimum, devastating.

Computer-related losses of money and information are more common, and they are much easier to deal with than missile losses. Money and information are regularly stolen, lost, or misappropriated in a manner that can be traced to actions involving the misuse of computer systems. Clearly, this loss potential will continue to grow as computers become the only practical method to control the collection, storage, and distribution or dissemination of these assets.

The losses that you can prevent are directly related to the assets that your organization controls with its computer systems. They can be the direct result of some intentional act, such as a theft. Certainly this was the case when a consultant stole more than $10,000,000 from a West Coast bank. From a practical viewpoint, however, most of your losses will be the direct result of an error or omission by someone on your staff.

Errors and omissions by your staff can result in losses because assets have left your organization; for example, losses that result from a defective check printing program. They can be losses in production time and expenses because work must be redone. They can be losses that result from actions that are initiated on the basis of incorrect information. They can also be losses that arise from the unauthorized disclosure of your information that either helps a competitor or results in a legal action against you.

You, and others in your organization, can reduce computer-related losses and loss potentials. It will cost the organization money. However, the cost of securing the organization's assets should not exceed the cost necessary to operate at a level of risk that management knowingly wishes to accept.

1.1.1 Misconceptions and Facts

There is a general public misunderstanding about losses resulting from the use of computers. It is important, therefore, to establish a practical perspective on computer-related losses by eliminating some myths and common misconceptions.

Misconception 1. Most computer losses are intentional.

Fact. Most computer-related losses are not intentional. They are the result of errors and omissions caused by members of the organization. The most common perpetrators are computer programmers, analysts and operators; data entry personnel who place wrong information into the computer; data gatherers who collect incorrect information; and personnel who incorrectly obtain or release information.

Determine if this is true in your organization by asking your audit, information systems and business managers where they find most losses are occurring.

Misconception 2. Most computer losses are large dollar losses.

Fact. Large dollar losses that involve computers are rarely reported. They make front page news occasionally, yet the average computer-related loss is quoted at $500,000. The evidence from computer fraud studies does not corroborate this, nor does it seem reasonable to conclude that there are large numbers of major computer criminals at this time.

Misconception 3. New laws are necessary to combat rampant computer crime.

Fact. Many states now have computer crime laws. Few attempts have been made to prosecute individuals under these statutes.

Legal changes may be necessary to deal with computer-related fraud and abuse. However, rather than create new laws, a better approach would be the redefinition of "property" to include information and computer services as tangible assets with provisions for attaching substantive loss values.

As an example, one computer-related fraud investigation that I participated in involved the demonstrated gain by the offenders of $43,000 from the sale of processing resources (computer time) to their customers, that they had wrongfully diverted from their employer.

That crime carried a maximum misdemeanor penalty of one year in prison. The perpetrators' biggest concern was an associated charge of possessing stolen property, a computer terminal worth a few thousand dollars, that could have resulted in a felony conviction with a prison term of several years.

Misconception 4. Computer security is a computer technician's problem.

Fact. The security and control of the organization's assets, including records and recordkeeping systems, is a management responsibility. Failure to comply with this responsibility can place top management in jeopardy from within the organization and from external regulating bodies.

1.2 HOW EASY IT IS TO BECOME A SECURITY FAILURE VICTIM

Your organization has probably been a security failure victim. The question is, "How much have you lost?"

Prior to becoming a computer security officer, I held computer-related positions in three large organizations. Two of those organizations had experienced computer security incidents resulting in losses that were quietly resolved without informing higher management because of their "trivial" nature. Top management never knew about the incidents, yet they were general knowledge to the data processing staff.

The actual monetary losses in those incidents were in fact small. However, the potential for substantial losses from the lack of appropriate controls was great. I continued to see and investigate similar incidents while I was at the Department of Investigation. I have no doubt that some managers would rather accept occasional losses than advise higher management of the security deficiencies that created the opportunities for employees to exploit the lack of appropriate controls. You may find it helpful to determine how losses are reported within your company.

The following list provides examples of loss situations that may be occurring right now in your data center and revenue collection departments:

- Loss of receivable income due to payments that are accidentally discarded
- Fraudulent or erroneous preparation of negotiable documents
- Improper disposition of computer equipment
- Theft or diversion of money and other tangible assets

– Theft or diversion of computer service

– Unauthorized alteration of official records

– Theft or unauthorized duplication of copyrighted programs

– Theft or misuse of confidential programs and information

– Theft of computer supplies

It is easy for your organization to become a victim of an intentional fraud. However, you are more likely to become a victim of errors or omissions. These commonly include the failure to:

– implement programs that hold individuals accountable for their mistakes;

– adequately test computer programs prior to placing them in production status;

– include adequate controls in computer programs because the end user or computer staff didn't think of them;

– include adequate controls in computer programs because they would delay project completion or computer operations;

– properly secure computer data and programs, resulting in the inadvertent modification or destruction of these assets;

– properly back up data so it could be easily replaced if damaged, destroyed, or misplaced;

– include adequate editing or error checking procedures within computer programs because these were planned as a data entry responsibility.

Many of the *failures to perform* described above could be blamed on the managers and technicians who were directly responsible. However, that would be both unfair and unreasonable if their management had not demanded better security procedures, controls, and advice about the vulnerability of their computer system to fraud, waste, errors and abuse.

You can make a positive difference in reducing your organization's vulnerability to computer-related asset losses by developing and enforcing realistic policies, standards, and procedures. Start by identifying the assets that your computer systems control, and then determining what victimization could cost your organization. Address the highest loss potential situations first.

1.3 WHAT VICTIMIZATION WILL COST YOU

Every computer-related loss that your organization sustains will have an effect on you and the organization. The consequences of the loss will depend on the size of the loss, what you did to prevent it, and its overall impact on the organization. You can begin to estimate the size of your loss potential immediately. (Chapter 8 provides you with a framework and a methodology for using these estimates to help you establish your security action plans based on the probabilities of these losses occurring.)

Two factors, as in the missile example earlier in this chapter, have a direct bearing on defining the size of the loss; the value of the asset, and the consequences of its being lost or misused. The value of an asset is easiest to define if it is money-related, such as a loss in a payables system.

As an example, we will determine the maximum loss that could occur in a payables system. The numbers are arbitrary and can easily be replaced by real values obtained from your organization. Assume that 1,000 payable checks are normally printed each day. The checks are imprinted on the face to indicate that they are not valid if the amount shown is greater than $2,500. Suppose the computer program that prints the checks were to incorrectly, by intent or error, print each check to the wrong payee in the amount of $2,500. The computer could then print $2,500,000 worth of erroneous checks, which could be directly mailed to the wrong payees. Some payees would cash the checks; others would call or write to advise you of the error. How much could you lose?

Using these arbitrary numbers, let us evaluate the potential loss in more detail:

–value of checks printed	$2,500,000
–% negotiated before notification and stop payment order	<u>50%</u>
–asset value at risk	$1,250,000

Some, if not most, of this estimated potential loss would be recovered, but the potential for a large loss is real.

Could this loss really happen to you? Probably not, if controls are in place to prevent it. These controls may include:

- careful testing of all computer programs before they are placed in production;
- controls in place to make sure that only qualified, authorized personnel make and place the properly tested changes in production;
- security systems that prevent unauthorized personnel from making changes to your programs or data;
- control totals that are prepared and checked before the checks are released for mailing.

Losses similar to this example have occurred to others, and they could possibly happen to you if your controls failed. Because this type of real dollar loss could happen, it is a prime candidate for inclusion in your list of exposures if you were to become victimized. Other errors and omissions, call them "goofs" if you prefer, are possible and they should be included. Consider some of the following examples in defining your loss potentials.

- Victimization costs that result in lost production time and materials. This can be estimated in real dollar losses by your operations staff. Request a list of all computer production runs that failed or were aborted. Your losses can be determined by adding up the costs of the resources consumed during the run (raw materials, supplies, machine time, personnel costs, etc.), subtracting any salvage value, and then adding in any costs of adjustment or consequent production delays or failures.
- Victimization costs resulting from a legal action that might be initiated against you because you failed to adequately protect information and someone's privacy rights were violated; or you improperly reproduced or divulged copyrighted computer programs.

As a last example to help you define what victimization will cost your organization, consider the problems that could arise if your computer system goofs and the wrong merchandise or information is sent to your customers. A major New York City bank mailed tax statements to its customers in 1984 that were incorrectly prepared as a result of a computer program error. A second mailing and a note of apology was required to remedy the problem. The losses in this example were direct rerun costs (computer time, supplies, postage, salaries) as well as customer dissatisfaction.

Intentional loss potential must also be included in your assessment of victimization costs. These are simply how much someone could steal from you if they wanted to, and if they had the ability and opportunity to do so. Money losses are again the easiest to define. The consultant who was mentioned earlier and his $10,000,000+ theft is the highest-ranking reported loss, but certainly bank wire transfer systems are potentially vulnerable to much larger losses than have been reported.

How many dollars could someone steal from your organization? In making your assessment, don't overlook the more probable and frequent minor losses that occur in an organization. They are the small embezzlements that can add up to thousands of dollars of loss to the organization each year. Donn Parker's book, *Fighting Computer Crime* (Charles Scribner's Sons, 1983) provides many examples, some amusing, that you may enjoy reading after your security program is in better shape than it is now.

The theft or misuse of computer data and processing services should also be included in your potential loss assessment. Your data, which include computer programs, formulas, and customer lists, may be very valuable to a competitor or a marketing research company. They should have a value associated with them for inclusion in your assessment.

Similarly, your processing resources are valuable. Computer time and data storage space are commonly misappropriated by employees. That costs you money. One estimate by auditors at a federal facility placed this loss at 3 to 5 percent of machine utilization and disk storage space. That could mean an annual loss of many thousands of dollars to a large organization if the same percentages are applied.

Losses resulting from goofs and thefts represent losses that are easiest to believe may actually happen to you. However, a third type of loss must also be included—loss of processing capability and data availability. Each year organizations suffer substantial losses as a result of a fire, flood, snowstorm, or some other form of catastrophe that destroys their data center. It doesn't happen often, but it does happen. This is the most extreme case of lost processing capability and data availability. More commonly, data or programs are damaged or destroyed because of equipment failure, human errors, and short-term disruptions. These are minor disasters, and an estimate for this type of loss also belongs in your cost of victimization.

1.4 HOW TO START AN EFFECTIVE COMPUTER SECURITY IMPROVEMENT PROGRAM

Security is a very easy area in which to evade direct responsibility—the "it didn't happen on my watch" syndrome. Unless the determination of responsibility is made part of the company's approach to security, much time can be wasted in trying to get things done or trying to determine why something went wrong. Start improving your security program by assigning responsibility for program improvement/development to a specific individual. Also, help that individual to start and continue building top management support for the whole security program.

Top management support will be the key to an effective computer security improvement program. The degree of support for adding security measures will be based on top management's interest and the perceived need for more security than currently exists. You may need to create that awareness and interest before you get the necessary support and resources to make significant changes.

Management interest in security increased considerably during 1983 and 1984. The impetus for this temporary increase in interest and level of perceived need was the widespread publicity that resulted from the successful penetration of computer systems by hackers. The hackers were primarily misguided teenagers who were able to access other people's computer systems.

Most hackers did not do substantial damage to the computer systems that they were able to invade. They were delighted merely to demonstrate their technical ability to log on to poorly secured computer systems, copy limited amounts of data, and then boast of their accomplishments to the media. The result was front page media attention and widespread public interest in computer security.

The kids were a boon to security officers and consultants. Resources were suddenly made available to make sure that corporate officers didn't have to be concerned about a front page newspaper picture of a grinning youth holding a printout of the organization's data. It should be noted that there is a clear difference between being able to log on to a computer system, and having a total breach of security where the individual who has logged on is able to access sensitive data or do consequential damage to the data. Both types of security breaches are bad, but hacker concern often resulted in resources being focused on the limited issues of outsider log-on control rather than on an overall program to prevent substantive losses that could result from knowledgeable insider actions.

You, absent continued hacker publicity, will be faced with the more common business problem of competing for resources with other managers. You will have to find the "hot buttons" that will work to get management to provide resources for security in your organization. Here are five suggestions that have been successful.

1. Present a Business Case for Security

Define what areas of security require improvement, what the exposures will be if the improvements are not made, and what will be required to reach a satisfactory level of risk acceptance. Methodologies for defining vulnerability and the consequences of vulnerability exploitation are presented in Chapter Eight.

The risk and vulnerability assessment provides a formal business case method to express your concerns and resource requirements. It can be used to get resources if your management understands and believes that a real potential for security-related problems exists. It may not be effective if your management does not understand or believe your assessment; if you cannot demonstrate that substantial problems have occurred; or if dollar value savings as a result of security improvements cannot be effected.

Substantiate your risk and vulnerability assessment with examples of security-related problems that have impacted your organization and show how the improvements that you are recommending will make a positive difference. Money losses and public credibility issues are usually most effective. They are easy for management to understand.

Major intentional losses will get management's attention and result in action, but fortunately they don't occur very often. However, when they do occur they get media and corporate auditor reviews that may result in immediate attention to selective security problems. Therefore, use any major losses to good illustrative advantage when explaining your funding needs.

Losses that can be prevented by better error and omission control or improved productivity can be used to justify security improvements. Prevention suggestions are presented throughout this book.

Minor losses, such as by employees who have been caught using the organization's computer for private business uses (frequently for consulting support or printing mailing labels) usually do not excite top management. They are perceived of as disciplinary matters to be handled by middle management or the security department. Minor losses may be useful in supporting your case based on other losses, but they should not be used as the sole basis for getting more resources from top management.

2. Plan to Build an Ongoing Security Program

Security programs, like any other business expense, need to be evaluated and modified on a basis consistent with the changing needs of the organization. There are few absolutes to dictate how much security may be required or how much security management will be willing to pay for at any moment in time.

The key to staying in control will be to develop a methodology to identify what sudden changes can impact security, requiring more or fewer protective measures, and a timetable to review those security measures that may not change dramatically. Again, there are no absolutes, but as a guideline, you should build security reviews into the application development and maintenance procedure to detect sudden changes, and coordinate periodic reviews and vulnerability assessments. (These are described in Chapter Eight, and as part of the EDP audit process.)

Federal government managers have explicit guidance with regard to reviewing their security programs by performing risk assessments. Office of Management and Budget Circular A-71, Transmittal Memorandum No. 1 (July 27, 1978), "Security of Federal Automated Information Systems" requires that risk assessments be performed:

(1) Prior to the approval of design specifications for new computer installations.
(2) Whenever there is a significant change to the physical facility, hardware or software at a computer installation. Agency criteria for

defining significant changes shall be commensurate with the sensitivity of the information processed by the installation.

(3) At periodic intervals of time established by the agency, commensurate with the sensitivity of the information processed by the installation, but not to exceed five years, if no risk analysis has been performed during that time.

3. Build Rapport with Your Auditors

Auditors, especially EDP auditors, are at times perceived as pests to be accommodated and deceived to the greatest extent possible. This is an unfortunate misconception and can work to the detriment of a well intended but underfinanced computer security operation.

You need support and the ability to communicate your requirements to top management. The auditor can be an effective conduit to communicate your needs and resource requirements to top management. You must lay the groundwork for this to happen. Facts and demonstrated cooperativeness on your part are essential. Review Chapter Six for some helpful hints before your next audit meeting.

4. Present Modular Work Plans

You will rarely get enough people and money resources to resolve all of the security issues that you believe are important. Also, top management may have different priorities than you have established at any particular time. Be prepared with a modular work plan that goes well beyond your current staffing and budget capabilities. Specify what your top priorities are and what you plan to accomplish at the level of staffing and funding that you are requesting. Demonstrate, in a language and presentation format that your management will understand, the benefits to the organization of meeting your priorities and objectives.

Be ready with a list of "also-do's" that would be beneficial if additional resources were approved. These second priority items, such as new physical access control devices, may be required now or at a future date, and you add to your credibility by preparing management well in advance of your formal request.

Finally, a ready list of also-do's should always be available in organizations that must spend all funds during a fiscal year or suffer a budget reduction in the next year. Contractors who do business with government organizations sometimes call the end of the fiscal year "wheel-barrow" time, and they are always ready with product and service ideas.

5. Stay Visible and Vigorous

Formal approaches may not be the best way to get and maintain your management's attention for needed security improvements. Your management may need to be educated and convinced by you and others, *many others*, within the organization. Start building grass-roots support by communicating at all levels within your organization. Issue regular progress reports and memos, in common English, to keep top management informed of your accomplishments. Concentrate on the benefits of the improvements that you keep making. They should be evident in increased operational control, reduced computer program maintenance requirements, fewer production program execution reruns, and better access to information. Here are a few suggestions:

- Develop and enforce security policies and procedures in a realistic and helpful manner. Don't expect all employees to be wildly enthusiastic about each new security improvement, but expect compliance and cooperation. Enjoy each genuine "thank you" that you receive when one of your improvements helps someone and that person takes the time to let you know about it.

- Purchase or prepare posters that offer security and safety suggestions. Place them in conspicuous locations and change them regularly.

- Publish articles or a security column in the organization newsletter. Keep stressing the objectives of security in terms that employees can relate to, such as improved access to needed information. Restricted access to information will not be perceived as a positive benefit.

- Hold regular security awareness meetings to reinforce the organization's commitment to maintaining and improving security. Stress the need for the active involvement of all employees in the protection of assets. Solicit comments and ideas from attendees. Act on the suggestions that you receive.

It is critical to your funding and ultimate success that you maintain security as a positive force within your organization. Computer security should be recognized as helping people get the information they need while protecting data and dollars from activities that would be detrimental to the organization. Keep sending positive reinforcement to all levels of the organization that your computer security unit is alive, well, and helping the entire organization.

Note: The manager responsible for developing a computer security program may find two case studies on this topic helpful. One describes the EDP security function in a banking environment, the other relates to a government setting. They are "Establishing and Managing an EDP Security Function," Sandra M. Mann, *Computer Security*, Computer Security Institute, Northboro, Mass., January/February, 1982; "A Strategy for Dealing with Computer Fraud and Abuse," Rolf T. Moulton, *Computer Security Journal,* Winter, 1982.

chapter 2
Key Control and Computer Security Concepts

This chapter describes the fundamental controls that should be present in computer application systems. It specifically deals with the individual and interactive contributions to security of people, computer programs, and security tools (devices). This chapter is more technical than most of the other chapters in this book and you may wish to reread it at a later time.

As you go through the chapter, try to relate the material presented to your computerized operations. Begin to look for ways to improve your systems; begin to look at your systems as they would look to a hostile adversary who would seek to benefit from the weaknesses of those systems.

2.1 UNDERSTANDING CONTROL CONCEPTS

2.1.1 Control Objective and Function

1. Control Objective

The objective of every control should be to prevent an undesired event from occurring, and/or to contain the impact of an undesired event to a predefined level of tolerability. The controls used in an automated teller machine (ATM) provide an example of controls that meet both objectives.

A. Prevention Example

In order to use an ATM, the prospective user must have both a valid card and a valid personal identification code before it will communicate. This first level of preventive control provides the means to identify the prospective user. Additional preventive controls involve specific computer processing procedures that come into play after user communication is established. They are discussed later in this chapter.

B. Impact Constraint Example

The prospective user of the ATM who has a valid card and a valid identification code may be an account holder at the bank or may have fraudulently obtained the card and identification code number. The ATM does not have the ability to distinguish between the two possibilities. In order to limit the impact of dispensing funds to an unauthorized individual, the ATM is programmed to dispense a limited amount of cash during any twenty-four hour period.

2. Control Function

A control function defines how the control meets its objective. Optimally, a control should:

A. Deter Intentional Attempts to Compromise the Control

Expanding on our earlier example, a card and code are required to get an ATM to dispense cash in the manner intended by the bank. This deters unauthorized use of the ATM by people who do not have a card and a code. Forcible attempts against the machine are deterred by conspicuously locating the device in a public area, and, in some cases, monitoring it with a camera.

B. Detect an Intentional or Unintentional Act or Event That the Control Seeks to Prevent

The ATM continues to serve as a good example. The computer program controls may not detect an unauthorized user who has someone else's valid card and code, and is attempting to initiate a fraudulent transaction. This detection could only occur if the card has been reported as being misappropriated. The computer programs could, however, easily detect a cardholder's attempt to withdraw funds in excess of balance availability because the ATM can have access to the user's account balance.

The ATM could also be designed to detect any physical attempts to compromise its computer controls by anyone tampering with its circuitry or protective casing. The detection control would be an intrusion alarm system.

C. Prevent the Undesired Action or Event from Occurring

Controls can directly prevent an undesired event from occurring after the attempt has been detected. Continuing with the ATM example, the machine will not dispense any cash unless it has validated both the user's identity and account funds availability.

It would be difficult or impractical to prevent all undesirable actions or events from occurring. Excessive cost of control and the need to conduct the business of the organization are the two most compelling reasons for not implementing computer system controls that exceed reasonability or cost-effectiveness.

D. Notify an Appropriate Function That the Undesired Event or Action Has Been Attempted or Has Occurred

This function is similar to that of an intrusion alarm. The alarm system cannot physically prevent a break-in, but it can provide notification that a break-in has been attempted. Similarly, some computer system controls serve a vital function by alerting the user that the action is incorrect and/or notifying a security officer of the attempted act or event, or its actual occurrence.

E. Provide an Audit Trail

An audit trail is a control that may be used to determine when and where an undesired event has occurred, and/or to enable investigators to determine the cause and perpetrator of the event. Audit trails may also be used to correct errors and omissions, and to recover data that has been damaged during processing.

2.1.2 Three Primary Computer Controls

1. Application Controls

The term APPLICATION has a very specific meaning when discussing computer systems. An APPLICATION PROGRAM is a computer program that addresses a specific user requirement. A check print program is an example of an application program.

An APPLICATION SYSTEM is one or more application programs and related manual procedures, which together meet a larger related requirement. A payroll system that processes time records, maintains payroll information, and produces payroll checks is an example of an application system.

APPLICATION CONTROLS are the manual and computer processing procedures that either prevent or limit the impact of an undesired event from occurring. They also verify the performance of a function as intended by management within an application program or system. An alternative term of an application control is a BASIC CONTROL.

An example of a manual application control in a payroll system would be having a clerk match employee time cards to a department master list to make certain that each employee had submitted a time card. An equivalent computer application control would be having a computer match each employee time record number that had been submitted to the master file of employee identification numbers to determine if all time cards were submitted.

The inclusion of application, or basic, controls is the direct responsibility of the application owner, such as the payroll manager. The application owner may request the assistance of the EDP auditing department in establishing which application controls are necessary. However, ultimately the payroll manager must be held accountable for the security of all payroll operations, both manual and computerized, without regard to who specifically is processing the work or how it is being processed.

2. System Controls

SYSTEM CONTROLS are those manual and computer processing procedures that protect the application controls from being compromised. The term INTEGRITY CONTROL may be used synonomously with system control. System controls are the joint responsibility of the EDP department and the application system manager.

The payroll example may be expanded to clarify the distinction between application and system controls. The application controls serve to ensure that the payroll records are processed in the manner defined by the payroll manager. The system controls, which are manual and computer procedures, deter or prevent unauthorized changes from being made to the payroll application programs and data.

The use of the term SYSTEM may cause some confusion for those people who are not accustomed to computer talk. This is especially true when it is used to describe programs. SYSTEM is used to differentiate between application programs and programs that are necessary to operate and control the computer. Programs that control the execution of the application programs are individually described as system programs or system software. The system programs are collectively known as the OPERATING SYSTEM.

The operating system programs schedule the execution sequence of previously submitted application programs, prevent individual application programs from invading each other, and perform many accounting and control tasks related to application program execution. Operating system controls are discussed later in this chapter.

3. Compensating Controls

COMPENSATING CONTROLS are those procedures (manual or computerized) that offset the need to have a control at the particular point during the processing cycle. In our payroll examples above, the clerk may have also checked for the completeness of information on each time card that was submitted. This task could have been performed at a later time, after the data was input to the computer, by the application program. The absence of the manual control would have then been compensated for by the presence of a computer program procedure control.

2.2 HOW PEOPLE MAKE THE SYSTEM SECURE

2.2.1 Multilayered Security

A computer security program is similar to a military security system. A layered approach with multiple controls is used.

Consider figure 2.1. A high fence with a limited number of guarded entry and exit points is the first layer of protection. Its function is to keep the general population (outsiders) at a safe distance. The guard and concerned staff are the first layer, or level, of defense or control.

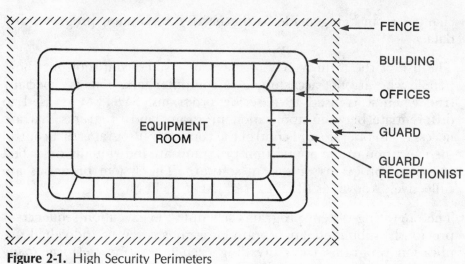

Figure 2-1. High Security Perimeters

The second layer of control is at the building level. People, guards, general staff, and sometimes barriers and equipment, are used within the building to further restrict access to sensitive areas to a limited number of personnel who have additional access authorizations.

The third layer of security is the knowledge or ability required to start the equipment, with or without the ability to make it do what it is intended to do. Recalling the extreme lost asset example in Chapter One, the accidental launch of a nuclear missile, it would be unfortunate to lose the asset. Two keys, at separated switches, are used to prevent unauthorized launch arming.

The fourth security layer is the knowledge required to use the equipment for a specific purpose. This is no longer a physical people control. A knowledge of procedures, codes, and so forth needed to use an application is required to initiate an unauthorized act or to improperly perform an authorized act. How well the act is prevented or its impact contained is now a function of the equipment or, in the case of an application system, the computer programs involved.

2.2.2 Specific People Control Concerns

People and procedures, as described in figure 2-1, were the initial security controls. The strongest technical or physical security program will fail if the people who are authorized to use protected resources and applications are compromised. Consider these four people security concerns that may be related to your computer security program before we move on to computer controls that can be used to protect computer systems:

1. Physical Access Control

Do your staff members provide an adequate level of physical access control to your protected assets? Specifically, do they prevent, or detect and report, attempts to gain access to computer programs and equipment that could compromise the integrity or continued availability of your data and processing resources?

The primary thrust of computer security was once directed at keeping unauthorized personnel out of the computer room. This changed as computer terminals extended the physical computer room to programmer and application user work areas. Physical computer security now includes the protection of the computer site, surrounding work areas, and computer terminals and communications networks.

2. Separation of Functions

Do you and your organization maintain an operating environment where sensitive data, computer programs, and transactions are restricted on a need-to-use basis; and so that collusive actions would be required to breach security?

Specifically,

- systems programmers should not have uncontrolled access to application programs or production data;
- application programmers should not have the ability to access or to modify system programs, production programs, or production data; and they should only be permitted to make authorized changes to application programs;
- computer operations personnel should only run programs and equipment. They should not have the ability to modify either programs or data.
- transaction initiators, such as clerks and bank tellers, should not be able to modify any computer programs. Their ability to input or modify data should be restricted to what management has defined as appropriate to their organizational function.

3. Application Access and Usage Control

Do your managers and staff members provide an adequate level of control with respect to how an application is accessed or used? Specifically, do they:

- develop effective application processing procedures?
- adhere to established procedures when they process input to applications, such as signature verification?
- each have a unique user identification number and password so that they can be held accountable for their application-related actions?
- develop application and system controls that record the transaction initiator's identification for each entry?
- protect their passwords? Passwords are not protected when they are conspicuously written down or shared with other staff members.
- protect application documentation? A trash rummager was one of the first computer-related criminals to make headlines. He succeeded in diverting substantial amounts of business equipment by using application documentation that was routinely discarded.
- report all application discrepancies or merely treat them as computer goofs that can be corrected? Computers rarely goof. Most, if not all, errors made by computers are errors made by people. Three basic causes of computer-related goofs are: incorrect input of data, incorrect computer programming, and improper data correction.

4. Application Output Control

Do you and your staff members adequately protect the information and documents that are printed or available from your computer system? Specifically,

- Are application programs developed so that sensitive information is protected at the data field level?
- Are sensitive reports destroyed rather than merely thrown in general trash bins?
- Are checks or negotiable documents handled correctly? We found very little technical computer crime in New York City

government. However, various types of prepared negotiable documents were stolen prior to being mailed or otherwise given to the rightful recipient.

People controls should be supplemented by application controls and security devices (equipment). However, even in a highly computerized application system, people controls are an important layer of security protection.

2.3 HOW COMPUTER PROGRAMS PROTECT YOUR SYSTEM

Computer programs protect application systems and operating systems by restricting system access; checking input data; verifying the results of data manipulations; preventing the unauthorized modification, destruction, and disclosure of data and programs; detecting and reporting attempts to compromise the integrity of data and programs; and by creating an audit trail of actions that were attempted or accomplished.

Effective program controls are extremely important in protecting the application and the system programs. Program controls have some advantages over people controls. They don't suffer from attention lapses; they do exactly what they are told to do; and they are not subject to human mistakes and vices.

Computer program controls do have some severe deficiencies though. Someone must include them. They must be absolutely complete. They require human follow-up. Their integrity must not be compromised for expediency or some other purpose.

2.3.1 System Access Overview

Figure 2-2 describes the layered interaction among computer program controls. The outer ring represents a combined teleprocessing network control system (NCS) and operating system (OS) which provides access to application programs. The functions of each of the programs within NCS and OS will vary depending on how the data center's staff designs and implements its programming. Therefore, it is easiest to refer to the controls that function externally to application controls as part of NCS/OS controls without differentiating which specific subring they are part of.

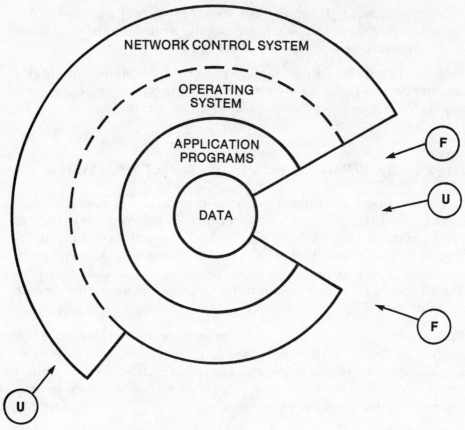

Figure 2-2. System Component Relationships

The application ring represents application processing programs and the controls that are part of those programs.

Data is at the center of the diagram. The data itself may be an asset or it may be the representation of an asset. Access to data is normally controlled by application programs. However, some NCS/OS programs have the ability to bypass application programs and access data directly.

The characters in the figure represent Friendly and Unfriendly forces which would attempt to interact with the data. Employees and clients who are authorized to use a system are generally classified as friendly. However, employees and authorized clients may attempt to exceed their authorization levels, or otherwise attempt to perform unauthorized actions, and hence can become unfriendly. Intruders are always unauthorized and are therefore always unfriendly.[1]

2.3.2 Computer System Access Controls

Computer systems may be accessed by dial-up telephone networks or by terminals that are directly connected (hard wired) to the computer's communications facilities. Using a terminal to communicate with a computer is defined as ON-LINE or INTERACTIVE PROCESSING.

Applications that process previously collected data are defined as BATCH PROCESSING APPLICATIONS. They do not normally require the same system access or log-on procedures described below as part of the NCS/OS security procedures.

A system user must pass through NCS/OS security to the application program level before a transaction, such as a payroll update, can be initiated. (See figure 2-3.) The system user does not have to breach

---

TYPICAL COMPUTER TERMINAL LOG-ON PROCEDURE

   1. Dial computer access number or turn system-connected machine on.
   2. Enter code for computer system to be accessed.
   3. Enter user identification number.
   4. Enter password.
   5. Enter code for application system to be accessed.
   6. Enter application password.

This is a typical series of steps that may be required to pass through NCS/OS security to a computer application system. Step 2, as shown, may occur after step 4, or may be omitted entirely. Its inclusion and placement is dependent on application system and operating system design criteria.

Note: Some application systems are designed to permit a user to log-on to the application system directly. This would eliminate steps 2 through 4.

Figure 2-3. Log-On Procedural Steps

---

[1]Moulton, Rolf T., "A Practical Approach to System Security Devices," *Computers & Security*, Volume 3, Number 2, May, 1984, p. 94.

application level security if the objective is only to use the processing resources of the system for some unauthorized activity, such as to commit a theft of services.

NCS/OS has many security controls to help authorized users and to prevent unauthorized access. These include:

Pre-Log-On Display Programs

The first security control that can be used for computers which can be accessed by terminals is the log-on display message. Overly friendly computer systems will display a company logo or some other identification to any user who dials the computer's access phone number. See figure 2-4 for an example of an overly friendly display. This is a poor use of the security that is available at the NCS/OS level. Authorized users will know who you are and how to log-on (establish communication) to your computer system. Unauthorized individuals who attempt to access dial-up computer systems are aided and encouraged by a display such as that shown in figure 2-4. Therefore, pre-log-on displays should be omitted or else contain only an indication that a connection to a computer system has been established.

Log-On Procedures

Computer system log-on codes and procedures (for terminal users) are the next security measure. They are necessary to gain access to a computer. They establish that the would-be system user is in fact an authorized user. Procedures needed to initiate a terminal log-on should not be displayed. (See figure 2-5.) The procedures should be contained in limited circulation documents.

The security terms used to describe what takes place during establishing a computer log-on session are identification and authentication. NCS/OS identifies who the prospective user is by matching the

```
 _____
|                              |
|        X Y Z COMPANY         |
|       NYC DATA CENTER        |
|_____|
```

Figure 2-4. Overly Friendly Pre-Log-On Display

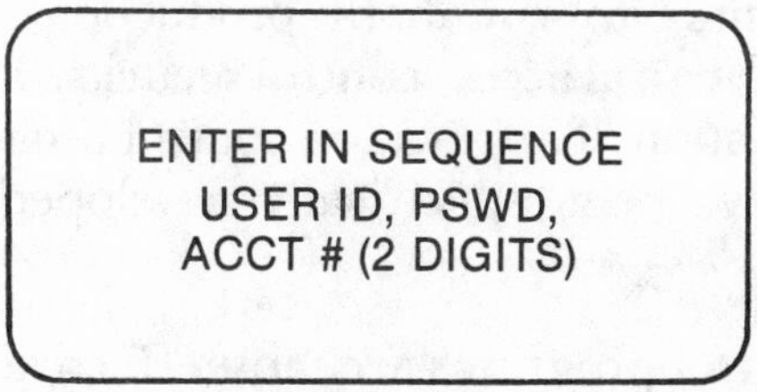

```
ENTER IN SEQUENCE
USER ID, PSWD,
ACCT # (2 DIGITS)
```

Figure 2-5. Overly Friendly Log-On Help Procedure

identification code (USER ID) entered by the user to a list of authorized system users which is stored in the computer's main memory. It will then proceed to authenticate that the prospective user is in fact who he claims to be.

The most common means to verify if the prospective user is a valid system user is using a password or a personal identification code. In the cash machine examples, a bank card and code are used together to perform identification and authentication.

Identification and authentication techniques are discussed in considerable detail in Chapter Four. At this point, however, it is important that the reader understand that some reliable means to identify and authenticate a user can, and should be, available for log-on access security.

2.3.3 Application System Access Controls

Once a person has logged on to a computer system, that individual is considered to be an authorized system user. Almost all controls that prevent further access to application programs and data will involve computer programs. At this point the distinction must be made between PHYSICAL ACCESS CONTROL and LOGICAL ACCESS CONTROL.

Physical access control is maintained when the user is physically prevented from gaining access to resources such as equipment, programs, and data. Keeping unauthorized personnel out of a computer room is one form of physical access control. Keeping a production computer system physically separated from a test computer system, and requiring a different access phone number, similarly provide physical access control.

Using one computer to run both production and test programs requires the use of logical access control security. This is accomplished by either a combination of application control programs or by NCS/OS programs that have been specifically developed to provide access control.

Logical access control programs are most effective when they are part of the NCS/OS software. They should be maintained by computer security officers, or else by operating system programmers rather than by application programmers.

The logical access control programs (software) can grant or deny access by individuals to specific application programs, such as payroll application programs. They can also restrict the access capabilities of individual application programs to specific data files. Some logical access control software can further restrict access to specific computer terminals which must be used to access application programs and data during predefined time periods.

Figure 2-6 represents the general process used by NCS/OS to control logical access to an application program. The application program is sometimes referred to as a SCREEN. If the user can access the screen, or the program that prepares and presents the screen, the user can normally execute the program(s) that will process the data which is input to the screen.

The authorized user's ID, with or without further password checking, and depending on which vendor product is used, is tested to determine if the application system may be accessed. If, as in the example, the user successfully passes all three access tests—application system, terminal ID, and application program requested—NCS/OS transfers control to the application system. If the user fails any of the tests, NCS/OS may allow a retry or initiate additional security procedures.

All system access attempts, successful or unsuccessful, should be recorded by logical access control software to provide an audit trail for management review. Access attempts that fail repeatedly may indicate a security problem, an equipment problem, or a lack of user training.

Application access to batch- or card-oriented computer production systems is protected in a manner similar to that used for the on-line transaction checking described above. The primary difference is that

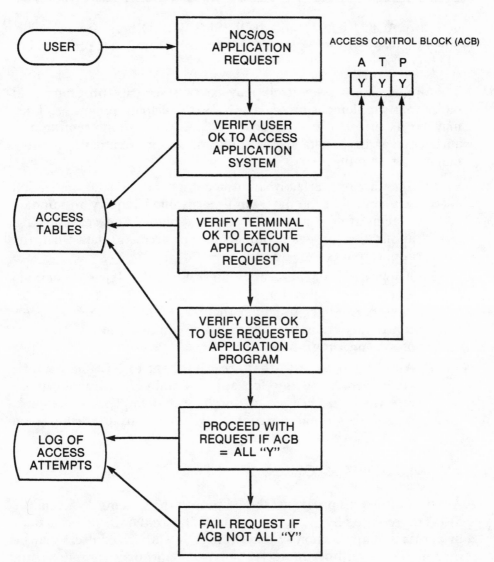

Figure 2-6. NCS/OS Logical Access Control

the logical access control programs verify information that is input in a job control card. The card reader which is used in batch program submission is the functional equivalent of the on-line computer terminal.

Logical access control programs may be obtained from specialized vendors and computer manufacturers. Three currently popular products are ACF2, RACF, and TOP SECRET. Others are available. Suggestions for using logical access control software are presented in Chapter Four.

The application system itself may contain security programs and tables that supplement or replace NCS/OS security programs. They may be as effective as the NCS/OS programs in preventing unauthorized access to data via the application. However, they have three major shortcomings:

1. They are only effective in protecting data while the application has control of the data. On-line customer inquiry and update systems are frequently shut down at night or on weekends. An application program cannot prevent access to data when the application is shut down.

2. Application system security controls are developed and implemented by application system programmers. This precludes the separation of functions that is present when logical access control programs are controlled by computer security officers or systems programmers.

3. Application controls that are equivalent to NCS/OS controls are expensive to develop and maintain. It is usually more effective and cheaper to purchase and implement standard NCS/OS logical access control products than to develop them as part of the application program.

2.3.4 Application Data Controls

Application system programs should protect the system's data, and the assets represented by the data, from unauthorized or incorrect actions by authorized application system users. The authorized users may be humans in an on-line interactive environment, or a computer program in a batch environment. Two important ways to control application data involve data editing and file updating.

1. Data Editing

Application program controls should verify that input data, which is entered to an application program, is valid and complete before it is used to update or modify other data. The process is known as input data editing. It may be performed at *character*, *field*, and *record* levels.

Character edits are performed first. The application program can check the value of each character of data as it is input, and take an action based on this test. The most common tests are made to ensure that numbers, letters, and special symbols are input in desired locations.

Characters are grouped into strings of characters known as "fields." The value of a field can be tested after all of the individual characters have passed an edit test.

Field values can be tested to see if they fall between an expected range such as 00000–88888 or AAAAA–CCCCC or they are equal to specific values such as dates or product numbers. They can be tested for their presence or absence; and they can be tested for duplication of entry.

An assembly of fields which are related in a meaningful manner is defined as a RECORD. After the fields in a record have been validated, the record may be matched to either a control table (list), or to the data base or master file(s). This control tests acceptability of the record by the application program or system. It may also prevent the omission or duplication of data depending on the logic of the update procedures that follow the input data verification steps.

The extent to which input data may be edited is limited by application system design. However, handling erroneous or incomplete data becomes more difficult the further it progresses into application program processing.

2. File Updating

Edited input data is used to update (modify, add or delete) a master file(s) or data base. Application design must include appropriate controls throughout the update process. These may include additional authorization tests, such as credit limit checks, and a logging of activities for both audit trails and program restart capabilities.

Computer processing of input data is similar to manual processing. The data elements may be immediately acted upon, stored for some future actions, or acted upon and the results stored in some modified form for future use. An on-line airline reservation system may serve as a better example than our payroll system. The application programs process a validated request for a ticket, a flight seat is reserved, a ticket is issued, money is received, and the entire series of actions is reconciled by the computer.

Airline ticket processing involves a series of complex processing procedures and controls. First, the flight file is checked for seat availability. A seat is booked only if seating is available. Then, a ticket is printed on a special form which either the computer or a reservations agent controls to prevent unauthorized use. Concurrently, the computer accounts for ticket money in a cash or a receivable account. At some point in the process, the computer programs reconcile dollars and people as flight revenue. Throughout this process, computer programs did, or should have, performed control procedures which prevented incorrect actions, reduced the impact of actions that were not prevented, and maintained a record of data and program activity for management's review and corrective measures in the event of an error or unauthorized action.

2.4 HOW EQUIPMENT PROTECTS THE SYSTEM

Equipment has always been an important part of every computer security program. Initially it was used to prevent physical access to computer rooms, and for fire detection and suppression purposes. Today, computer security equipment can also be used to prevent access to computer resources as well as to protect data while it is being transported by communication links to and from data centers.

2.4.1 Data Center Security

1. Physical Access Control

Physical access control equipment is readily apparent in most large data centers. It starts with a lock on the main door and continues with alarms on the emergency exit doors.

The doors that provide access to the data center are the primary barriers to unauthorized access. They must be sufficiently strong to deter unauthorized forcible entry.

The locks on the doors are as important as the doors themselves. Conventional key locks provide an adequate level of security for small computer rooms where very few people are permitted access. They are not adequate for large data centers where many people are permitted access.

Large data centers should have door locking mechanisms which require, as a minimum, the possession of an object, such as an ID card, and possibly the knowledge of a secret code. These modern systems have the ability to restrict access to authorized individuals at specific entrances during specified hours of selected days. They are readily available and work well when used in conjunction with proper people controls.

Card access systems can also be used to log each entrance and exit attempt. This capability makes them useful for time and attendance systems as well as for providing an audit trail of who was in a particular work area at any time. A card access system with extensive reporting capabilities may cost $100,000 or more for a large data center.

Alternatives to card access lock systems are available. These include hand geometry identification, palm and finger print recognition, voice authentication systems, and tiny radio transmitter systems. The alternative systems may be more appropriate for some operations, but this would depend on the level of security required and the additional price management is willing to pay for physical security.

2. Fire Safety Systems

Fire detection equipment should be present in all large data centers. Large data centers, and their associated equipment and supplies areas, normally contain many millions of dollars worth of computer and communications equipment and data. Providing an adequate level of fire notification for staff safety and equipment safety is absolutely essential.

The need for fire suppression equipment is not as clear-cut an issue. Local building and safety codes may require a minimum level requirement for suppression devices such as Halon gas systems or water sprinklers. Where a choice of equipment may be made, consider the following practical realities before making your selection:

    A. Value of your data and equipment.

    B. Presence of personnel on a twenty-four hour basis.

C. Remote locations, such as tape vaults, with unattended operations usually should have fire-suppression equipment.

D. Response time from local fire departments.

E. Effectiveness and cost of the alternatives.

2.4.2 Computer System Access Security

1. Dial-Back and Dial-Through Devices

Computer system security devices are available that make unauthorized dial-up access almost impossible. The most effective devices are dial-back devices.

Dial-back devices are placed in a computer system's telecommunications network. An individual who wishes to access a computer by dial-up telephone calls the dial-back device and enters his user identification number, usually with touch telephone or a Touch-Tone generator. The user then hangs up or otherwise disconnects the phone line.

The dial-back device then checks its internal list of authorized user IDs and the days and times that the system may be accessed by the user. If the user meets the authorization criteria, the dial-back device then calls the user at the phone number where it expects the user to be. The authorized user may then begin the log-on procedure.

Dial-through devices, some of which are dial-back devices with this added capability, provide the same user identification as dial-back devices. However, a dial-through device accepts a password or other code, and then, after authentication, passes the call through to the computer system. Both dial-back and dial-through devices may provide an audit trail of successful and unsuccessful access attempts.

2. Test and Diagnostic Equipment

Computer and communications test and diagnostic equipment play an important role in ensuring the integrity and continuity of data services. Much of this equipment is not normally considerd as security equipment. Rather, it is sold for quality control purposes.

However, test and diagnostic equipment has serious security implications when it contains user identification codes, passwords, and data encryption and decryption algorithms. Consequently, the equipment must be appropriately safeguarded and its usage controlled.

2.4.3 Communications Link Security

1. Link Protection

A communications link is necessary to connect distant computers and terminals. The terminals may be standard "dumb" terminals, "smart" terminals that have limited processing capabilities, microcomputers, or remote job submission stations.

The link may directly connect the terminal to the data center. Coaxial cables and twisted pair wires are commonly used to "hardwire" terminals to computer systems. Beyond a few hundred feet, terminals must be connected by means of a communications link such as those listed below. Specific link vulnerabilities are included. "A Practical Approach to System Security Devices" provides the following description of link vulnerabilities and data protection recommendations:[2]

> *Dial-Up Lines* have the lowest level of security protection. Anyone with a terminal or microcomputer can attempt network access for inquiry or update. Line taps are possible.
> *Leased Lines* have a higher degree of security because they are physically attached to equipment and can be uniquely identified. Line taps are possible. (Dedicated lines under user control have the same problems as leased lines.)
> *Satellite Transmissions* are extremely vulnerable because anyone with a "dish" can intercept or initiate communications.
> *Miscellaneous Links*, which include fiber-optic and microwave circuits, offer distinct security advantages. Fiber-optic lines are very difficult for an intruder to compromise and may become a major security improvement device.

2. Data Protection

The data on the link may require protection beyond the quality controls that are provided by line test and error-checking hardware and software. The link may be compromised by direct tap or other signal interception. If this occurs, data may be obtained without the owner's authorization, or unauthorized transactions may be initiated by a network intruder. Therefore, if the integrity of the link cannot be guaranteed, the data on the link must be made unusable to the link penetrator.

Encryption, which many network users unfortunately think is synonymous with data security, is a very powerful tool to protect data

---

[2]Moulton, Rolf T. "A Practical Approach to System Security Devices," *Computers & Security*, Volume 3, Number 2, May, 1984, pp. 93–99.

while it is on a communications link. It should be considered for networks where security requirements are high, and where its use is not precluded by regulation or national law.

Encryption is the "scrambling" or recoding of data prior to transmission so that intercepted data will be meaningless to the link penetrator. Encryption may be performed by either hardware or software devices. The original data to be transmitted *(cleartext)* are converted into an unintelligible form *(ciphertext)* prior to sending. The ciphertext is sent to its destination where it is translated back into cleartext. The process is referred to as encryption and decryption.

Encryption is not a new technology; computers just make the process easier to use. The encryption process is controlled by an algorithm and a key. The algorithm is the method by which the data is scrambled. The key is the means to start and stop the scrambling in a manner which makes the data useable to the keyholder.

The National Bureau of Standards developed the Data Encryption Standard (DES) which provides a method of encryption which has not been broken to date. Other less rigorous methods have been proven as breakable. The DES has been implemented in both software and hardware devices.

The choice of encryption implementation should be based on network design, cost of operation, and host processing capability. Software encryption devices require CPU cycles from either the network or the host CPU. Hardware encryption devices use their own CPUs and do not impact host CPU performance, but hardware-implemented encryption requires a larger initial equipment cost than software encryption.

Key management is a significant security liability with encryption. Care must be taken to ensure the secrecy of key distribution and storage. Similarly, communication diagnostic equipment which contains keys must be protected.

chapter 3
Defining Your Computer Security Responsibilities

This chapter will help the reader to define his responsibilities for the protection of the organization's assets. It deals with operational security, legal requirements, and organizational policies—which may or may not exist.

It will present those changes to security requirements that have resulted from the concentration and processing of information by computers. A checklist is included to help the reader define the specific security responsibilities which he may wish to assume or to delegate to others.

3.1 HOW COMPUTERS AFFECT YOUR OPERATIONAL SECURITY

3.1.1 Why Operational Security Has Changed

Operational security is achieved when a manager is in control of the assets for which he is held accountable. Absolute operational security, if at all possible, may not be achievable at a cost commensurate with the value of the assets that are at risk. Therefore, organizations establish policies, standards, and procedures to maintain what they believe is an adequate level of control.

The assignment and acceptance of responsibility for asset control are critical security factors. Assuming responsibility for physical assets is a relatively easy task. Items like inventory and cash are visible. They are routinely recorded. They can be counted and reconciled on any basis of frequency that management feels may be necessary to assure a comfortable level of control, thereby assuring that an operationally defined level of security exists.

Assigning and assuming responsibilities for controlling the ownership, collection, storage, use, availability, transmission, and dissemination of computerized data is more difficult to accomplish than for physical assets. Consider that computerized data, which is both an asset and the representation of other assets, may not be under the full control of one business group or manager because it may be:

– "owned" by one group;

– processed by a different group;

– reproduced, stored, and used by one or more different groups.

Computerized information may also be:

– modified or updated by one or more entities with different reporting relationships;

– copied, modified, or disclosed without the knowledge or consent of the owner;

– unavailable if normally used processing equipment or computer programs are not operational.

Three examples are provided to illustrate how your operational security has changed in a computerized environment.

Example 1: Program Change Control

A brief overview of computer program preparation is necessary at this point. Computer programs are written in specific languages such as COBOL, BASIC, or RPG. The program, as written, is referred to as the source program or source code.

The source programming language is essentially computer independent. The same source program could be used on IBM, Burroughs, or Digital Equipment computers without major modifications.

A source program must be compiled or translated into the language required by a specific computer before it will operate or execute. The compiled version of a program is referred to as an object program or object code.

The object code is modified further prior to execution by a process known as link editing. However, it is not necessary to understand this step to illustrate the control deficiencies presented in figure 3-1.

Figure 3-1 illustrates the typical way that a large organization may control access to its computer programs. The master copies of all source programs are stored in libraries that are maintained for each "owner" department. Owner departments, for this example, include Payroll, Accounts Receivable, Purchasing, and so on. A programmer who needs to make modifications to a computer program copies the source code for the program into her personal library. The programmer then modifies and tests the program copy in her library. When the programmer is satisfied that the changes are ready to be placed in production, she compiles the source code program into object code and places a copy of the object code into the production test library. The programmer also copies the revised source code into the master test library.

The programmer fills out a program move form, which is approved by the Programming manager, to advise the production control function to copy the revised source program to the master program library and to copy the revised object program to the production library. Production Control performs these copy requests on a weekly basis.

The program modification (maintenance) cycle for this organization is now completed.

The flow of events seems orderly and logical. However, for this hypothetical organization, it lacked the controls necessary to protect the operational security of both the application owner and the Data Processing department. Let's expand on the illustration and look at both the control deficiencies and reasonable methods to improve security.

1. Master Source Library

Deficiency. Programs in the master source library were available on a read-only basis to anyone in the organization who was authorized to use the computer system. This was done because restricting access would have

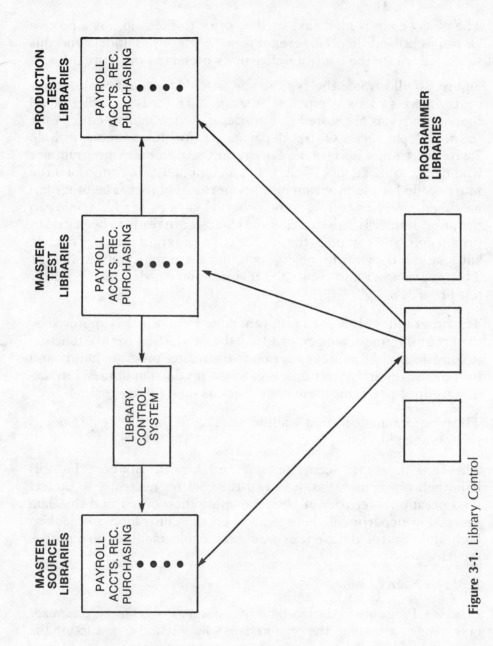

Figure 3-1. Library Control

required an increased administrative overhead on the part of Production Control, and the organization had never had a reported security-related problem with its programming staffs.

Remedy. Access to source programs should only be on a need-to-know basis. Production Control should make copies of individual programs available to programmers only when directed to do so by an appropriate manager.

2. Programmer Libraries

Deficiency. Programmers in the organization commonly share passwords to their personal libraries with their co-workers. Programming management felt that the sharing was beneficial for productivity until one programmer became disgruntled. Then management began to wonder if that programmer might try to make unauthorized modifications to other programmer libraries.

Remedy. Hold programmers individually accountable for protecting their passwords and programs. Strictly control any sharing of libraries that may be absolutely essential for any particular programming assignment.

3. Master Test Library

Deficiency. Access to the master test library was controlled by a password. Unfortunately, the same password was used to control all test libraries. From a practical viewpoint, therefore, any programmer, or former programmer, could modify or delete any program in the master test library without management's or Production Control's knowledge.

Remedy. The master test library is a staging area for programs that are to be placed in the master source library. Develop a procedure to control transferring programs into the master source library.

4. Production Test Library

Deficiency. The production test library was not password protected. Any authorized computer system user could recompile a test program into that library without management's or Production Control's knowledge. Production Control could move an incorrect program into production status.

There was another vulnerability in this production test library. Programmers were occasionally allowed to execute test programs against

live data when severe program problems required immediate attention, such as late at night and on weekends. These test production
emergencies did not require management's approval.

Remedy. Two immediate actions are necessary to correct a situation like
this:

1. Source programs should always be compiled into production
   object code by the Production Control function. This will help
   to ensure that the production source program and object
   program are the same program, and that the program is the
   one approved by management.
2. Test programs should not be executed against live data, and
   especially not late at night or on weekends. Operating this way
   bypasses all management controls.

On those rare occasions where a nonproduction status program must
be executed against live data, always require that the programmer's
supervisor be contacted for prior approval. This will improve control
and magically reduce the number of emergencies.

The example presented above describes an operational security situation that may be almost invisible to you as a manager who relies on
computers to process a daily workload. It may seem more like a
theoretical problem to be addressed by the Data Processing department or the EDP auditors. However, it is your problem if it ultimately
impacts the security of your operations.

Example 2: Payables Fraud the Old Way

Consider another typical operational security situation that may relate
to your organization—the control of payables. Payables are a high
vulnerability area for intentional fraud because payable systems
provide a means to generate checks. They also represent an area of
high vulnerability where errors and omission can cost your company
real dollar losses and staff time losses, as well as embarrassment when
incorrect checks are sent to vendors or customers.

The payables process starts when an organization places an order for
goods or services. The order may be entered into your computer
system to anticipate the expense, or a copy may be manually filed. At

some point an invoice is received and a decision is made to make payment.

The invoice payment process in a large organization is almost certainly a computerized process, even though the ordering procedures may be only partially computerized. There are two common computer-related ways that employees beat payable systems: (1) manipulating the paper-work prior to entry into the computer system, and (2) changing data after it has been entered into the computer system.

The manipulation of payment documents may include the modification of legitimate invoices, as well as the introduction of bogus invoices. One former government employee, who later also became the former employee of two large companies, found it very easy to modify payment documents. His methodology serves as a good example. Let's call him Mr. C.

Mr. C worked as an input clerk in a payment processing unit. Data entry clerks in that unit entered approved payment information into the payables system from forms prepared by various departments in other agencies.

Mr. C simply modified the payee name and address on one form to a fictitious company at his home address. It was easy to do. The forms were left in unattended boxes and no one noticed his activities.

Mr. C then placed the altered form back in the box. It was entered into the payables system by an unsuspecting clerk. The payables system remained in balance because the dollar totals were the only reconciliation factor.

Unfortunately for Mr. C, the system had other controls. The input form was returned to the originating department. There, a clerk was responsible for matching the forms to a printed listing of checks to be issued. The originating department's clerk noticed the change to the input form and called for help.

Mr. C was surprised to find detectives photographing him and his mailbox. He was able to escape and deposit the check, but he was soon apprehended and convicted. His sentence for the $5,000 fraud was five years in prison, but he was placed on probation as a first-time offender.

Mr. C went to work for two other companies. The first company merely fired him when he was caught changing payment forms for his own benefit. The second company fired him and had him arrested. He was convicted and sentenced to a prison term.

The payables system controls worked against Mr. C at all three organizations. Would a similar scheme be detected at your company?

The operational security of payables systems can also be compromised after data has been input. Many organizations do an excellent job of controlling both the anticipation of invoices and the entry of payment data. Changes to documents, such as those which Mr. C made, would be readily detected. However, a security failure can occur when any computerized name and address file is not properly protected. Let's examine this further in Example 3.

Example 3: Payables Fraud the New Way

It is advantageous in the design of large systems to have data files that serve many functions. As an example, the vendor name and address file for the payables system may also be used for the purchasing system. It may also be accessible by other departments' employees. The security issue hinges on the question of who can change the name and address file.

Let's consider a hypothetical Mr. N who is able to modify vendor name and address records in the computer system. Also assume that Mr. N understands how the payables system works and can read and modify the data in it from his own or from someone else's computer terminal.

Mr. N looks at the payment files to determine which checks are to be issued and when they are to be issued. (Normally payment data is entered some time in advance of check issuance and an automated cash control function of the payables system issues checks at the last possible date.) He selects the victim payee and changes the payee's name and address to his own. The system issues the check on the specified date. Mr. N, knowing how the system functions, then changes the payee name and address back to the originals.

Would your organization's system know the difference in time to prevent check issuance in the above scenario? Would you have an adequate audit trail to determine what happened, and to catch the perpetrator?

3.1.2 Five Ways to Immediately Improve Operational Security

Here are five preventative security measures that will reduce your vulnerability to fraudulent actions by employees:

1. Run a Background Check on Employment Candidates.

Conduct a thorough review of a prospective employee's past employment history before he is hired. Mr. C, in the example above, had been convicted of a felony, yet two employers had apparently missed that fact.

2. Restrict Access to Your Systems.

Access to computer systems should be restricted to those individuals who need that access to perform a job function. Chapter Two describes several methods for restricting access, but of greater importance is determining who needs that access and why they need it.

Identifying an individual's business access requirements to computer equipment, programs, and data should be relatively straightforward. The key criteria are the business need for the individual to have access to the resources in question, and the losses that could be sustained by intentional or accidental modification, destruction, or disclosure of the resources.

Personal use of the organization's computer equipment, programs and data should not be permitted. It may lead to loss of data and other abuses.

Consider data vulnerability as an example. The computer systems store the company's information treasure. Would the organization encourage or permit its employees to keep personal records in the sensitive central filing systems? It is highly unlikely. Why should computer filing systems be treated any differently?

You may wish to liken a computer system to a vault. Would the organization permit an employee to keep personal funds in the organization's vault? Again, it is highly improbable. A computer system that administers millions of dollars in payable and receivable funds is a very big vault.

You may not agree with this restrictive philosophy of computer security and may want to make some limited processing capability available to employees on a management discretion basis. In this situation, it is recommended that appropriate policies be developed to ensure fairness of access by the employees, to define which resources may and may not be used, who may use the resources, and that appropriate accounting and auditing procedures are developed and implemented to control personal use.

3. Log and Examine Changes to Production Data.

Data that has been previously entered may require changes and corrections. Log these changes in a manner that will enable a control staff to review the authenticity, as well as the accuracy, of the changes.

4. Check Your Records Retention Cycle.

Review your computerized and manual records retention cycle to make sure that it is adequate for operational recovery purposes as well as for fraud detection and recovery. The Data Processing department can help you with operational recovery planning. Check with your Auditing and Security departments on records retention to combat fraud.

5. Evaluate the Disruption Recovery Contingency Plan.

A new operational security concern is your ability to continue meeting your mission if your company's computer systems are not available when they are needed. You probably know how to cope with short-term computer system outages. They are becoming less common for well-designed systems but they do occur occasionally. What would happen if your computer center were to be totally destroyed?.

The total destruction of a computer center is a rare occurrence, but it does happen because of fires, floods, earthquakes, and the like. How would your operations be impacted if your organization's computer center were to be destroyed or to otherwise become unavailable? Chapter Ten discusses disruption recovery. If your company's disruption plan doesn't seem adequate, start improving it.

3.2 HOW YOUR ORGANIZATION'S SECURITY POLICY AFFECTS YOU

The presence of a clear, unambiguous computer security policy will help you as a manager by:

    – defining your responsibilities;

 – defining the responsibilities of the various departments in the organization that may impact or evaluate the security of your operations;
 – providing notice to all employees that they have a security responsibility.

3.2.1 Your Responsibilities

Your security responsibilities are easier to discharge if you know what they are. A policy statement provides this guidance. The absence of a policy statement leaves you with unspecified responsibilities that will become relevant at the most inopportune times, such as when a security incident occurs, or during an audit.

An organization's security policy may only provide general guidance for managers. Specific statements of responsibilities may be contained in policies or directives issued by other high-level officials, such as a comptroller or a financial vice president; or specific responsibilities may be contained in standards or procedures issued at the organizational level.

Use whatever guidance your organization provides to help protect you from unpleasant surprises. Don't expect 100 percent security. It can't exist in a real world. A reasonable, cost-effective security program based on your organization's policies, however, can be achieved if appropriate policies exist.

3.2.2 Others' Responsibilities

A computer security policy will, or should, define the responsibilities of other officials and managers in your organization. As an example, the Audit department may be delegated the responsibility for issuing control guidelines or standards for computer security.

Knowing the guidelines and standards that you will be audited against will help you. You will know what constitutes a reasonable level of control in your organization.

Ask other organization officials, such as the comptroller, security manager, and audit manager, for help in locating policies, guidelines, directives, and standards that may be relevant to the security of your operations. You may also need assistance in interpreting how they apply to your operations.

Use the materials that have been prepared by others in your organization to help you to understand and evaluate the security risks that exist in your operations. You may also wish to use them to substantiate your decisions to implement or omit selected security controls.

3.2.3 Employee Responsibilities

This handbook will repeatedly stress the need to advise all employees of their responsibilities with regard to security. All employees may not need to know detailed standards and procedures for preventing computer-related losses. However, they need to know and should be held accountable for understanding the organization's policy(s) with respect to security.

You, as a manager, must make certain that your organization's concern for security and control is brought home to every employee. The first step in meeting this responsibility is to make sure that each of your subordinates has been given a copy of the organization's security policy, and that each one understands it.

Prepare and distribute a policy for your department if an organization policy doesn't exist. It will communicate both your concerns and expectations. It will eliminate the painful consequences that arise when a security-related incident occurs and you are faced with a "you didn't tell me"/"you should have known" situation.

3.3 HOW LEGISLATION AFFECTS YOUR RESPONSIBILITIES

Federal and state legislation and regulations affect the information that general businesses collect, retain, and disseminate. Some industry groups, such as banking, health care, education, for example, are specially regulated. The business manager responsible for developing and using computer systems needs a broad understanding of the issues involved so that she can seek specific guidance from appropriate organization management. Failure to comply with recordkeeping requirements jeopardizes both the organization and the individual manager.

Here are three legal areas that are essential to be aware of and to seek guidance on from your management.

3.3.1 Foreign Corrupt Practices Act (FCPA)

The Foreign Corrupt Practices Act of 1977 amends the Securities Exchange Act of 1934. It makes the payment of bribes to foreign officials unlawful and requires the maintenance of accurate records. Controlling the bribery of foreign officials is beyond the scope of this handbook, but let's look at the ACCOUNTING STANDARDS SECTION of the Act.

> (2) Every issuer which has a class of securities registered pursuant to section 12 of this title and every issuer which is required to file reports pursuant to section 15(d) of this title shall—
>
> (A) make and keep books, records, and accounts, which, in reasonable detail, accurately and fairly reflect the transactions and dispositions of the assets of the issuer:
> and
> (B) devise and maintain a system of internal accounting controls sufficient to provide reasonable assurances that—
> (i) transactions are executed in accordance with management's general or specific authorization;
> (ii) transactions are recorded as necessary (I) to permit preparation of financial statements in conformity with generally accepted accounting principles or any other criteria applicable to such statements, and (II) to maintain accountability for assets;
> (iii) access to assets is permitted only in accordance with management's general or specific authorization; and
> (iv) the recorded accountability for assets is compared with the existing assets at reasonable intervals and appropriate action is taken with respect to any differences.

The federal government has made it very clear that a company that falls within the Act's definition—and it applies to domestic corporations as well as those in foreign trade—must maintain accountability of its assets as reflected by its recordkeeping systems. Compliance requires adequate controls and a security program to ensure that the controls work. Failure to comply with the FCPA subjects the company to a maximum fine of $1,000,000.

The FCPA also has a personal liability for company officials or stockholders acting on behalf of company officials, who willfully violate the Act. They are subject to a maximum fine of $10,000 and up to five years in prison.

3.3.2 Privacy Legislation

Privacy legislation affects the computerized collection, maintenance, and transfer of personal information. Five major federal information privacy statutes exist as law: the Fair Credit Reporting Act, the Fair Credit Billing Act, the Privacy Action of 1974, the Family Education Rights and Privacy Act, and the Right to Financial Privacy Act of 1978.

John C. Lautsch, who was the chairman of the Computer Law Division of the American Bar Association Section on Science and Technology in 1984, presented many of data security management's privacy law concerns in his article *Privacy Law and DP Management.*[1] In that article, Mr. Lautsch lists nine principles that data processing management can use to gauge the acceptability of operations in terms of information privacy. They are:

- Openness principle. The data system and its policies and practices should not be secret.
- Individual access principle. The data subject should have access to information about himself.
- Individual participation principle. The data subject should have a right to correct and amend the substance of personal information about himself.
- Collection limitation principle. There should be limits on the type of personal information that can be collected, and on the manner of collection.
- Use limitation principle. There should be limits on internal use of personal information.
- Disclosure limitation principle. There should be limits on external disclosures of personal information.
- Information management principle. Recordkeeping organizations should bear responsibility for adopting practices to ensure that the collection, maintenance, use, and dissemination of personal information are necessary and lawful and that the personal information is current and accurate.

---

[1]John C. Lautsch, "Privacy Law and DP Management," *Data Security Management* (82–04–09), Copyright 1984 Auerbach Publishers Inc., Pennsauken, N.J., pp. 9–10. Used by permission.

- Accountability principle. Recordkeeping organizations should be accountable (liable) for their information practices.

Failure of the organization to properly protect the rights of people about whom information is collected can result in direct losses to the organization. Properly protecting information requires the implementation of reasonable safeguards. Mr. Lautsch further advises that:[2]

> Recent cases indicate money damages cannot be awarded for failure of a DP operation to comply with information-handling statutes, such as the Fair Credit Reporting Act. In *Bryant* v. *TRW Inc.*, a home buyer sued because a credit reporting agency caused the denial of a home loan after supplying inaccurate information to a mortgage company. The loan was eventually approved but only, the plaintiff testified, after embarrassment, anxiety, humiliation, and emotional stress. The Sixth Circuit Court held that "liability does not flow automatically from the fact that a credit reporting agency, such as defendant, reports inaccurate information…. Instead, liability flows from failure to follow (1) reasonable procedures (2) to assure maximum possible accuracy of the information (3) concerning the individual about whom the information relates…. (The standard of conduct by which (a court) must judge the adequacy of (consumer reporting) agency procedures is what a reasonably prudent person would do under the circumstances." The court awarded the plaintiff $8,000 in damages and also required the defendant to pay the plaintiff's legal fees of $13,705.

3.3.3 Tax Law—Records Retention

The Internal Revenue Service has its say in how companies should keep records. Two specific references that relate to management's security responsibilities for records retention follow.

> Adequate record retention facilities must be available for storing tapes and printouts as well as all applicable supporting documents. These records must be retained in accordance with the provisions of the Internal Revenue Code of 1954 and the regulations prescribed thereunder. (IRS Revenue Procedure 64–12)
> It is held that punched cards, magnetic tapes, disks and other machine-sensible data media used for recording, consolidating, and summarizing accounting transactions and records within a taxpayer's

---

[2]*Ibid.*, pp. 9–10.

automatic data processing system are records within the meaning of section 6001 of the Code and section 1.6001–1 of the regulations and are required to be retained so long as the contents may become material in the administration of any internal revenue law. However, where punched cards are used merely as a means of machine-sensible records, such punched cards need not be retained. (IRS Revenue Ruling 71–20)

The IRS requirements are only the beginning. One recent publication advertises that it contains "over 1500 specific records retention requirements." Bryan Wilkinson, in his article *"File Retention and Backup,"* recommends the following course of action to ensure effective file retention and backup:[3]

- Determine file exposure.
- Determine the government record retention requirements that affect the organization.
- Compare current record retention standards to exposures and requirements.
- Identify and evaluate local recovery problems and their solutions.
- Review the organizational understanding of potential recovery problems, proposed solutions, and legal requirements for record retention.
- Inspect and evaluate off-site storage.
- Review off-site storage agreements.
- Inspect and evaluate the facilities used to transport files to the off-site location.
- Determine special file access restrictions.
- Evaluate the usability of backup files.
- Prepare recommendations based on reviews and evaluations.

3.3.4 Summary Recommendations

Managers who develop and maintain computerized information systems have an obligation to understand the specific laws and regulations that apply to those systems. Failure to do so may subject the organization and the individual manager to criminal and civil prosecution.

---

[3]Bryan Wilkinson, "File Retention and Backup," *Data Security Management* (82–04–08), Copyright 1984 Auerbach Publishers Inc., Pennsauken, N.J., p. 8. Used by permission.

Company management, which includes the Legal and Auditing departments, must play an active role in reviewing what information systems are used for and how they accomplish the company's goals. The following are offered as general guidelines:

1. Develop information systems that collect, store, process, and disseminate only that information which is:
   a. required for the conduct of the business and;
   b. permissible to collect, store, process and disseminate by law and industry regulations.

2. Develop and maintain an adequate level of control within information systems to ensure that the information collected is accurate, current, and protected from unauthorized access.

3. Develop and maintain an adequate level of control within information systems to ensure that personnel who are authorized to access information systems do not intentionally or unintentionally damage, wrongfully disclose, or destroy the information that they are authorized to use.

4. Develop and maintain systems that will ensure that records are retained for periods of time that comply with government and industry records retention requirements; and that the manner in which the records are stored will ensure their security and availability.

3.4 HOW TO DEVELOP A SECURITY RESPONSIBILITY CHECKLIST

You, as a manager, are, or should be, held accountable for the assets that are under your direct control and those that belong to others but that you use. This is especially true, but not always apparent, with information processing systems.

Most users of information processing systems see a representation of data in a printed or displayed form. They rarely touch or physically modify the data or programs that modify the data, although micro-computers bring the action to a much more personal level of control.

Understanding your responsibilities for computer-related security requires understanding which computer systems you and your staff interact with and what is being done to protect them. A checklist will help you to define your responsibilities. Review the general suggestions for checklist items that follow. There are also general and specific management responsibilities that you can follow up on immediately.

3.4.1 General Responsibilities

1. Policies/Standards/Procedures
What/how does your company hold you responsible for:
- general responsibilities?
- specific responsibilities?

2. Staff Training
What is each employee expected to do and not to do?
How well does each employee know how to perform computer-related responsibilities?
How does each employee keep current with responsibility and procedural changes?

3. Systems Design and Operation
Which systems are you responsible for?
Which systems do you use that are not yours?
Are you satisfied with:
- operational performance?
- controls within the systems?
- controls that protect the systems?

4. Auditability and Control
How do you ensure the integrity and quality of your computer operations?
How would/could you follow up on a security incident?

5. Disruption Contingency Planning
Have you identified which application systems and programs are critical to your operations?
How well are you prepared to cope with critical system failures?
How well is the Data Processing department prepared to ensure the continuity of information systems that are necessary for your operations?

3.4.2 Specific Responsibilities

1. Data Capture
Are you responsible for the collection of data which is input to a computer system? This might involve point-of-sale terminals or

hand-prepared invoices that are later key punched.
How do you prevent errors from being recorded?
Are you responsible for reviewing data collection forms that are prepared by other departments?
How do you detect and correct previously recorded errors?
How do you compile and report an error rate report?

2. Data Entry

Are you responsible for entering data into a computer system in either an on-line or a batch environment?
How do you control the receipt of input documents?
How do you control the delivery or release of input documents after the data is entered?
How do you control the delivery of data that has been prepared for input?
How do you protect input documents from unauthorized changes, disclosure, and destruction?
How do you ensure that the input equipment is functioning properly?
How do you control the accuracy of input operations?
How do you record and report errors found in input documents?
How do you control and record errors made by input operators?
How are input errors that are discovered during later processing reported to you?

3. Computer Programming—Applications

Are you responsible for application program development and maintenance?
What/who initiates a request to design or redesign a system?
Is there a formal procedure for designing a system?
Who is responsible for enforcing system design procedures and standards adherence?
Are all program changes logged and reviewed?
Are programming errors detected?
Are all program failures logged and reviewed?
How do you ensure that only authorized program changes are made?
How do you ensure that the authorized changes work properly?
How is source/object code synchronization controlled?
Do you allow programmer access to production data?
Who maintains test data?
How is access to production source code maintained?

Do you rotate program maintenance responsibilities or allow assignment of programmers to specific systems?

Are detected program errors logged and reviewed?

Are off-site copies of program documentation maintained?

Are programmers allowed to use "ZAP" utilities?

How is the use of test time controlled?

How is the personal use of the computer controlled?

4. Computer Programming—Systems

Are you responsible for system program development and maintenance?

What degree of control can be maintained over systems programmers?

What/who initiates a request for a system programming change?

Are all vendor supplied changes reviewed?

How are vendor supplied changes controlled?

How are system libraries protected?

Are all changes to system programs logged and reviewed?

Are programming errors detected?

Are all programming errors logged and reviewed?

Are off-site copies of documentation maintained?

How is the use of "ZAP" utilities controlled?

How is the personal use of computer time controlled?

5. Computer Operations

Are you responsible for computer operations?

How well is physical access control maintained?

How effective are emergency procedures?

Are emergency contact lists current?

How well are housekeeping tasks performed?

Is the fire detection system adequate?

Are fire detection and suppression systems tested regularly?

Are all staff members familiar with first aid safety procedures?

Are program failures logged and reviewed?

Are operations errors logged and reviewed?

Is equipment adequately maintained?

Are equipment failure rates acceptable?

Does an adequate separation of functions exist?

Are performance targets met?

Are there special procedures for handling sensitive reports?

Is confidential waste adequately protected?

Are late shifts adequately staffed and supervised?

Is smoking restricted in the facility?

6. Data Communications

Are you responsible for data communications?

Is physical access control to equipment adequate?

What is the backup to the communications system network?

How is equipment selected?

What is the reporting relationship between data communication, voice communication, and data processing?

Who or what organization installs and maintains communications equipment?

How and when is the network configuration evaluated and changed?

How is network performance measured and reviewed?

How is quality of service defined and measured?

Does line monitoring and other test equipment contain or have access to encryption codes and passwords?

How is line monitoring and other test equipment protected?

7. EDP Disruption Recovery Contingency Planning (DRCP)

Are you responsible for EDP disruption recovery contingency planning?

Have critical application systems been defined?

How would critical applications be processed if a major data processing service disruption were to occur?

Is the DRCP tested regularly?

Is the off-site data and documentation storage facility adequate?

Is the off-site data and documentation storage program adequate and audited regularly?

Have you inspected the off-site data and documentation storage facility recently?

Do you believe that DRCP would adequately meet your operational needs?

chapter 4
How to Control Computer System Users

This chapter presents end user security problems: who is using the computer and how is it being used? It provides practical considerations for applying security technology in an organizational environment where added controls may seem more of a burden than a blessing.

The key concepts to look for are the methods used to positively identify who is using a computer system, what the common concerns for security include, and the practical realities of implementing security measures.

4.1 IDENTIFYING WHO IS USING YOUR COMPUTER

Large computer systems are designed to permit concurrent use by many people and programs. At any one instant there may be hundreds, and possibly thousands, of users. It would be comforting to believe that all the users were authorized users, performing authorized actions, in the most productive manner possible. However, this may not be what is really happening.

Consider computer usage in an office environment. Most employers tolerate a limited degree of personal use of office copiers, typewriters, and telephones. Computers, especially those used for the development of computer programs, are similar to any other form of office equipment. The first steps should be to define what the computers are to be used for, who is to use them, and how to control that use. (See Chapter Eight for policy suggestions.) The next step is the identification of who is really using your computer.

4.1.1 Identification

Two issues are involved in identifying who is using your computer system. The first issue is identifying who is currently authorized to use your system. This may be accomplished by matching, preferably by computer, a file, or list, of all people who are authorized to use your organization's computer to the various files, or lists, that indicate the current status of those individuals.

Performing this match may lead you to find that among your authorized computer users are terminated employees, transferred employees, and customers who have closed their accounts. This commonly occurs because paperwork lags behind actual events. It represents a very real vulnerability to every organization. You may wish to identify within your organization if any of those active but no longer authorized accounts are in use, as well as what each of them could do to harm your organization.

4.1.2 Authentication

The second issue is evaluting the adequacy of the controls used to determine if the computer processing accounts that are authorized for use are actually being used by those individuals who are authorized to use them. This is a matter of identification versus authentication and may be handled by the network control system or the operating system, as discussed in Chapter Two.

This problem is described succinctly from a network perspective in *Design Alternatives for Computer Network Security*.[1]

---

[1]Gerald D. Cole, "Computer Science and Technology: Design Alternatives for Computer Network Security," National Bureau of Standards Special Publication 500–21, V1, 1978, p. 11.

If a network is to provide controlled access of requestors to resources, the control mechanisms associated with these resources must have some way of determining and verifying the identity of the requestors. We use the term identification to mean the process of determining who or what an entity claims to be, and refer to the process of verifying this claim as authenticating (e.g., by using a password). The security aspects of concern are primarily those of authentication, since identification problems tend to be based on operational issues (e.g., whether Social Security numbers should be used as identifiers).... All entities which can affect security must be uniquely identified and authenticated. In the most straightforward case, an entity would have a globally unique name and an appropriate authenticator.

A description of commonly accepted user authentication techniques is provided in "A Practical Approach To System Security Devices."[2]

Password
The most common form of user authentication is a password. Passwords should be unique, changed regularly, protected during distribution, maintained in secure secrecy, and should have no inherent meaning, such as a nickname.

Passwords must be required at the initiation of each terminal session. They should also be reinput to the network on a predetermined basis to be sure that the individual is still the system user, and prior to initiation of higher-vulnerability transactions. Passwords and user challenge procedures should be built into the network security program(s).

Possessed Object
The use of a possessed object in combination with a password increases authentication capability. A magnetic stripe card and a physical key for locking the terminal are two common possessed objects.

Executing a transaction at an automated teller machine is an example of a password and possessed object combination. The bank card is used to initiate communication with the teleprocessing network by identifying that a user is present and that he claims to be a specific customer. The personal identification number (PIN) of the user serves as a password to authenticate the user. Once the user is identified and authenticated, the specific application program, in

---

[2]Rolf T. Moulton, "A Practical Approach To System Security Devices," *Computers & Security*, Volume 3, Number 2, May 1984, pp. 93–99.

conjunction with the user's authorized privileges, may initiate transaction activity.

Possessed objects have an inherent liability in that they may be lost or stolen. Prudent security, therefore, requires that their purpose not be identified, and that users exercise due care for their protection and report losses immediately.

User Attribute

User authentication by physical attribute can be combined with passwords and other secret "knowledge." Hand geometry readers were among the first of this security device type. Hand geometry has been used primarily for access control to secured areas rather than for individual computer terminal users.

Signature verification and fingerprint readers have also been tried. Each has a distinct limitation. People who do not sign their names frequently have a high rejection rate by automated signature verifiers. This limits their applicability when dealing with the general public. Fingerprint verification has technical problems and widespread public distrust which make it impractical for many applications.

Device Location

User authentication may be accomplished by restricting individual access to specific telecommunications equipment which is located in a secured area. This requires the ability of the network to identify and authenticate the transaction device(s) and assumes that appropriate people and physical controls are in place to deal with user authentication. The typical example of this technique is a data entry operation. A practical hardware location identification device for portable equipment is an automated dialback unit. The terminal user dials the network, inputs a user identification code and then disconnects the circuit. The dialback unit then calls the user at the location where the user is expected to be. This device may be used together with an embedded chip to further identify and authenticate the device. User identification and authentication procedures should supplement this hardware device.

Device location authentication has many limitations. Sensitive transactions need additional network controls. Application controls, discussed later, should always be imposed when device location is a primary authentication method.

Identify and Authenticate the Transaction Device

The transaction device can be identified by an embedded chip or by the line number of the dedicated circuit used. However, microcomputers can be used to emulate embedded chip identification. Therefore, additional security devices should be considered when using transaction device identification and authentication.

The use of dialup lines, especially by programmers at off-site locations and at their homes, should be controlled by a combination of location, device and user identification and authentication techniques. This is both possible and economically feasible using the methods described above.

4.2 UNDERSTANDING THE USER'S CONTROL AND SECURITY REQUIREMENTS

4.2.1 Defining the User

A user, for the purposes of this chapter, is defined as the manager of any area of responsibility that is dependent on computer processing to meet the objectives of her area of responsibility. Typical users by this definition would be a payroll manager, accounts receivable manager, airline reservations manager, and the like.

4.2.2 Common User Concerns

A security group comprised of user representatives at one organization described its security concerns as indicated below. They are fairly typical of the concerns raised by users, rather than those raised by computer security officers and EDP auditors. The concerns were:

accidental data damage;

stolen/copied data;

adverse audit reports;

lost assets;

downtime;

field level data access control.

1. Accidental Data Damage

Data which the user depends on is normally in the care and custody of the EDP department. The user rarely gets to see where the data is stored. It is stored and processed by the EDP department which has care and custody responsibilities. Even if the user could see the media (common computer tape and disk) on which the data is stored, the data would be invisible to the naked eye. Consequently, the protection of the data should become a high priority for the user who cannot directly protect that data.

For the same reason, accidental damage to that data is also a concern of the user. Sometimes, intentional data damage may be reported as accidental. This may occur because it is often easier for Data Processing management to treat the damage as accidental and unravel the mess without involving the user.

Accidental data damage can be traced to equipment failures or human errors. A good disaster contingency plan is the key to dealing with data damage, but let's look at the causes from a user's viewpoint.

Equipment failures are the easiest to understand. Consider media (tape and disk) in this classification. Data damage can occur during processing when a computer tape breaks, but, again, this rarely happens. More commonly, the tape becomes defective in one or more places because the iron oxide, which is the recording surface, wears thin or falls off. This concern is easy to resolve by periodically testing computer tapes on tape certification devices, and replacing defective tapes.

Disk drive and disk media failures similarly rarely occur. Disks are better protected than tapes because they stay mounted in one drive, which is more reliable than tape drives. Disks and disk drives should be periodically inspected and given routine maintenance.

Accidental damage to data caused by human error can be more difficult to control than equipment or media failures. The damage can occur as a result of a computer operator error or a programmer error.

Tapes are most susceptible to operator damage. They can be dropped or mounted as output instead of input. Rollaround racks can be used to reduce the number of dropped tapes. The use of a good tape management system should reduce the incidence of incorrect tape mounts resulting from human error.

Damage to data by programmers, including operations job setup personnel, can occur if the wrong data, either input or output, is specified. This vulnerability is substantially reduced with logical access control software, which is described in Chapter Two. The logical access control software protects data on both tapes and disks from being specified improperly.

2. Stolen/Copied Data

Data can be a very valuable asset to steal in its entirety or to copy for some unauthorized purpose. Stealing an organization's data and holding it for ransom has occurred in Europe. Holding data for ransom does not appear to be a problem in the United States. In the 1970s and 1980s, data and programs were being copied to avoid purchasing of programs, and for industrial espionage purposes in the United States. This is a very valid user concern and should be addressed with the log-on and access controls which are described in Chapter Two, and organization policies that prohibit the unauthorized copying and use of computer data and programs.

3. Adverse Audit Reports

User concern for control and security can be stimulated by adverse audit reports. The audit reports can identify weaknesses in both the user's area of responsibility and in the EDP department. The EDP manager can be of assistance to the user in resolving both types of control and security weakness.

Commonly reported user deficiencies include failure to properly segregate duties, improper error reconciliation procedures, an excessive number of people in authority, poor procedural controls, failure to require the use of access control software, and so forth.

EDP weaknessess that result in unfavorable audit reports may include absence of logical access control software, inadequate disaster contingency recovery plans, poor off-site data and program storage procedures, lack of data management systems, and improper segregation of functions within the EDP department, and so forth.

4. Lost Assets

Lost assets, as differentiated from damaged or stolen assets, can occur because computer programs or personnel fail to process transactions properly, or they can occur because data security controls are bypassed.

Direct user involvement in program development and testing, and in the development and enforcement of procedural controls, can reduce the user's concern with regard to the processing of transactions. Again, logical access control software can play an important part in limiting which users can access both sensitive data and sensitive transaction programs.

The loss of assets can be the direct result of improper EDP actions. One financial organization that I am familiar with "lost" several millions of budgeted dollars because a programmer failed to correctly restore data to a disk pack during a minor disruption recovery. Be sure that disruption recovery plans call for a log of all data and program-related activities.

5. Downtime

Users are concerned that their data processing related operations must always be available. The thought of resorting to outdated, or nonexistent, alternative processing capabilities is not appealing. Watch what happens when an airline's computer reservations system doesn't work for a few minutes and the result of machine dependence becomes obvious.

Your concern as an EDP manager, or as a user manager, should be the continuity of computer system operations. Multiple, redundant, central processing units can be used to prevent noticeable downtime. The use of dual processor central processing units provides a similar degree of protection.

Designing applications that can function at a local level on smaller processors is another viable alternative. This method can contain disruptions to local areas rather than affect the whole organization.

The choice of the specific strategy to reduce downtime disruptions and downtime losses must be based on the potential losses to the organization and the costs of prevention. This is discussed in greater detail in Chapter Ten.

6. Field Level Data Access Control

Users should be able to limit access to their data to the field, or individual data element, level. This concern would have been difficult to address in the 1960s and 1970s. It is not difficult to achieve in the

1980s. The key to resolving this concern is user involvement in application systems design, and the use of logical access control software.

4.2.3 Additional User Concerns

1. EDP Management Attitude and Responsiveness

EDP management must be responsive to user control and security requirements. The trend in some organizations to staff applications development and programming at the user level is, in part, a direct result of past failures to adequately communicate needs and solutions.

Dispersing data security administration to the user level can provide a good means to initiate cooperation where it does not currently exist. Dispersed security administration helps the user to understand what data and programs belong to him. It also positions accountability where it can be most effective.

2. Review of Obsolete Application Systems

Maintaining obsolete application systems is less risky, from a conservative EDP manager's viewpoint, than replacing them with new systems because their major flaws have usually been fixed. Unfortunately, older application systems frequently were designed for operational expediency rather than from a control and security perspective. This is discussed in detail in Chapter Seven.

Both user and EDP management should review application systems on a regular basis to determine which systems present operational and security vulnerabilities that could be reduced or eliminated with new systems development. This is especially important in organizations where microcomputers are or could be introduced into communications networks and where dialup access to production computer systems is available.

3. Training in Control and Security Practices

Training in control and security practices has not been a part of user or EDP training. This places both user and EDP staff members and management in positions of reliance on EDP auditors for service and comments on control and security matters. It is a philosophy that cannot work.

User and EDP management must compel staff members to attend courses that will provide a basis for understanding what can be done to improve systems design requirements to include adequate controls and security. They must also enforce getting those control requirements implemented in properly designed systems.

4.3 APPLYING LOGIC AND TECHNOLOGY TO PRACTICAL REALITIES

4.3.1 People, Programs, and Equipment

People, computer programs, and equipment provide three different techniques to achieve effective control. There are no absolute answers as to which one of the three can be used most effectively to obtain the highest level of security. Most large computer applications will require all three.

The key to establishing maximum security is identifying and quantifying potential security vulnerabilities during the system planning and design process, and then applying those controls that will keep losses within the limits defined by business management. Adding security to existing systems may require redesigning the system.

The distinction between technological security devices, both computer programs and equipment, is changing and will continue to change as new products are developed. The term "security device" may be more appropriately used to refer to either security programs or equipment.

4.3.2 Interfacing Security

The balance between using people controls and security devices will continue to shift towards computer-related controls and security devices. This is because technological security solutions are often more cost-effective than people solutions. However, people must interface with and use computer systems; so, cost-effectiveness and people usability become practical concerns when attempting to get the most effectiveness from security devices. "A Practical Approach to System Security Devices" summarized interface concerns as:[3]

---

[3]*Ibid.*, pp. 93–94.

Inclusion—The security devices should be incorporated into the network, application and system as part of the initial design process. This may not have been done and the devices must then be considered as "add-ons" to existing security measures. Add-ons cost more money than "designed-ins" and may not be as effective, but add-ons may be the only way to reduce security vulnerabilities until the system is redesigned.

Performance degradation—Security devices will require CPU cycles as well as additional manual procedures.

Cost—The devices will cost money to implement and maintain.

Degraded mode operation—Provisions must be made for continued processing if a device failure occurs. Applications may have to be run at facilities which are not compatible with the organization's security devices or operating system.

Device dislike—System users may not like the security devices. Some devices will add formality and extra work steps which may be a nuisance. Employees may seek ways to beat the devices as a means to increase their productivity or to perform some legitimate task which is prevented or restricted.

Device gameability—"Beating" the security devices may offer an intellectual challenge. Employees or other users may seek to compromise the device "for the fun of it."

Violation handling—Security violations (intentional, unintentional, system induced) must be anticipated. Procedures to deal with the violations and violators must be in place prior to device implementation.

Multilevel control—It may be necessary to have multiple levels of controls for a particular application. The device under consideration must support this requirement.

Device maintenance control—Personnel will be responsible for implementing and maintaining the devices—typically systems programmers. In addition, some devices, such as test equipment, may be capable of compromising other devices or controls. Therefore, control over test equipment and personnel will be a critical consideration.

Device implementation—Devices may require full implementation at a specific time. Others may permit installation by individual application or user location. This may impose severe training and implementation problems where multiple data files, large numbers of application users, or many user locations are involved. Device engagement can be particularly difficult when it is retrofitted rather than installed as part of the initial application implementation.

Exception accommodation—It may be necessary to bypass the security devices as a result of an exceptional condition. This may compromise other devices and controls.

chapter 5

Establishing More Efficient Controls Over the EDP Department

This chapter is directed to the manager who has responsibility for data processing applications but does not have computer operations responsibility. It discusses security from the viewpoint of a non-technical manager who must rely on the EDP department for systems development and implementation. It provides suggestions for getting the message "build more secure systems with my help" to the EDP department. (It may be redundant for data processing managers.)

5.1 UNDERSTANDING THE EDP DEPARTMENT'S MISSION

The mission of every EDP department should be to provide information services in a cost-effective, controlled manner. The mission of some EDP departments may also include ownership responsibility for the organization's data and programs. However, control is improved when the EDP department, rather than the owner, is the custodian of data and programs.

Data and program ownership should reside with appropriate organizational units. As an example, payroll data should be "owned" by, or under the direct control of, the payroll department. Similarly, the application programs that process payroll data should be owned by the payroll department. Appropriate ownership of data and programs increases the ability to control and audit the use of these assets and is discussed in more detail in the next section of this chapter.

The manner in which the EDP department meets its mission has been changed significantly by technology and business needs. Three basic models for providing information processing services have emerged. Some organizations use parts or all of the three basic models.

1. Centralized Data Processing

The traditional data processing department processes all of the company's data. Major equipment is consolidated under the control of the EDP department at one or more locations. Computer system users are provided with processing services that may or may not be charged to their budgets.

The central EDP department is responsible for the design or purchase of all user application systems. This does not preclude having a user or committee approach to the evaluation of systems development or acquisition. Nor does it preclude active participation by the user in the systems development or acquisition process.

EDP auditing may not have played an active role in the centralized data processing department's activities until the 1970s because few of the organization's general auditors understood EDP activities. During the 1970s, a change was apparent and EDP auditing began to emerge as a force for the EDP manager to be concerned with.

2. Service Bureau

A service bureau maintains EDP facilities and sells processing services and technical support to its customers. The service bureau concept became viable as large multiprocessing computers and high-speed data communications equipment were developed. Some organizations have developed their own internal service bureaus. Other organizations purchase processing services from independent service bureaus.

Using the service bureau's processing equipment may eliminate the need for the organization to maintain its own computer; the service bureau may only be used for development of new application systems; or the service bureau may provide processing power to supplement in-house computer services.

The organization that uses a service bureau may choose to retain all application program development; use technical services and application programs developed by the service bureau; purchase application programs from an outside vendor; or use some combination of these different approaches.

The role of the user organization's audit department within the service bureau model may be essentially unchanged from the central EDP department. The level at which specific audit activities are conducted, however, will depend on whether an in-house or an outside service bureau relationship exists, and the audit provisions of the service contract.

3. Decentralized Data Processing

Some organizations have decentralized, or dispersed, data processing equipment and applications development to user or business groups. This approach may result in large end user computer operations. It may also include smaller computer centers that are linked to each other and/or to a central computer which is maintained by the headquarters data processing department.

The advantage of decentralized data processing is that it provides a better opportunity for the users to control their own data processing priorities. The disadvantage is the potential for redundant application program and data development which may not easily interrelate with other programs and data within the organization, as well as a lack of relationship to the overall organization's goals, objectives and standards.

Auditing data processing activities in a decentralized environment will vary in effectiveness depending on the extent of decentralization, ownership of data and programs, end user sophistication, and the auditor's role and staff capabilities.

The personal mission of your EDP department's staff members will be related to the mission model(s) chosen and the allegiances of the EDP staff members. Large central staff EDP department members may consider themselves as part of the data processing profession first, the data center staff second, and the organization last. This loyalty sequence is easiest to understand where highly educated and skilled personnel are involved. They are very much in demand and their mobility and earning power are dependent on staying current with the technology that is their business rather than on the technical aspects of the business itself.

The mission of an EDP department staff that is highly integrated into the business will more likely be the support of the organization. The individual staff members may be less specialized and technical than large central staff members, but resulting applications may be more on target and have a better potential for including controls.

The potential for better application controls is greater where the application developers are less concerned with elegant technical solutions and more concerned with meeting the needs of the business. Adequate controls are certainly a business need. They weren't invented by auditors. They were created by business managers who wanted the business to remain viable.

The formal mission of every EDP department should be to provide information services to the organization in a controlled manner. This ideal will not be translated into reality at the practitioner level if you do not apply constant pressure to make it happen.

5.2 UNDERSTANDING HOW TO COMMUNICATE YOUR SECURITY REQUIREMENTS

You must thoroughly understand your control and security requirements before you can communicate them to the EDP department. Remember, you, not the EDP department or the auditing department, will or should be held accountable if your application systems fail to produce what is required in a timely and controlled manner. Here are four suggestions.

1. Review Your Application Data and Program Ownership

You may own or share the data and programs that comprise your application systems. You must know the status of each data file and program in your application systems before you can effectively communicate your security and control requirements.

The ease with which you will be able to determine the ownership of your data files will be related to the security administration of your data. If your organization is directly responsible for logical access control, a situation where you grant or deny access to your data, it will be very easy to determine what data you own. If you do not directly administer your logical access control, it may be more difficult to determine data ownership.

Determining data ownership in circumstances where centralized data administration exists can be easy or difficult. Don't be surprised if a "data administrator" or a corporate administrative function owns your data. Conversely, don't be surprised if the ownership of your data is unclaimed.

Similarly, someone must own the application programs that process your data. You must find out whether it is you or some other organizational entity. Program ownership, like data ownership, may be directly related to data security administration and/or data administration. It may also be a function of the organizational entity that prepares and maintains the computer programs.

2. Review Application Objectives

You will need to understand the objectives of each application system before you can understand the adequacy of the application's controls. The objectives of an application are the specific functions that are to be performed. A payroll system can serve as an example. The major objectives might be to:

A. Collect hours worked for each employee on a daily basis.

B. Prepare a weekly hours worked summary for supervisory review.

C. Prepare a weekly payroll check for each employee.

D. Prepare weekly tax reports.

E. Prepare weekly cost accounting reports.

F. Prepare monthly salary and tax summaries.

   G. Prepare quarterly salary and tax summaries.

   H. Prepare annual salary and tax summaries.

3. Review How Well Each System Meets Its Objectives

Once you understand what an application system's objectives are, you can begin to evaluate how well it meets those objectives. Review these operational requirements with your staff, and then with your organization's data processing manager:

   A. Do the outputs (reports, checks, data files, and such) from each of your application systems meet your requirements?

   B. Are exactly the right numbers of outputs created? Having too many copies of reports printed causes both security and wasted resource problems. Similarly, unneeded or unused reports are both security and wasted resource problems.

   C. Is each output (report, check, and such) produced on schedule?

   D. Is each output correctly balanced by the application programs or are manual error corrections (reconciliations) required? Who performs the error corrections if they are required?

   E. Are programs rerun or delayed because of "bugs" that resulted in a job failure? If so, who fixes the bugs?

   F. Are program changes required to keep the programs working? If so, how are you informed?

   G. Do programmers or operations staff run error correction programs to remedy or correct "bad" data files? If so, how are you informed?

4. Review How Well Each System Meets Its Control Requirements

You may require the assistance of an EDP auditor to review the control requirements of each application system. However, asking for an internal EDP auditor's assistance may be the same as requesting an audit (which could seem like asking for the kiss of death). Therefore, the practicality of requesting this assistance will depend on your evaluation of the EDP audit department's mission. (See Chapter Six.)

It may be more realistic to have one or more of your staff members take EDP auditing courses so they can act as your own internal audit function. Two weeks of training can open the minds and eyes of receptive individuals. Big 8 accounting firms and professional groups such as the EDP Auditor's Association offer excellent introductory courses.

The key controls to look for are:

A. Separation of Functions—Your Department

Are the activities that your staff members perform relevant to the application sufficiently separated and checked by other staff members and computer programs so that errors and omissions will be detected as early as possible? And so that collusive actions by employees and/or outsiders would be required to perpetrate a fraud against the organization?

B. Separation of Functions—EDP Department

The controls that are present in your computer programs must be protected by the integrity controls that were discussed in Chapter Two. This requires an appropriate separation of functions in the EDP department. Does it exist?

C. Individual Accountability

Errors and omissions will occur in any operation. Does your application system give you the ability to pinpoint the occurrence and the cause of every goof or intentionally wrong entry or procedure— human as well as computer program—within an overall effective security program?

D. Continuity of Operations

Computer services may temporarily cease to be available. Does you data center have a plan to deal with service disruptions? Do you have an alternative interim method of meeting your department's mission, which may include manual procedures, until computer services are restored?

In summary, the key to communicating your control and security requirements to the EDP department is prior research and understanding. Specifically, you must:

1. Understand your control and security requirements.
2. Understand the role of the EDP department and its relationship to you.

3. Understand the mission of the EDP audit department.

If you are satisfied that you have an acceptable level of control and risk in your EDP-related operations, you should let the head of EDP know that you are satisfied.

If you are not satisfied that you have an acceptable level of risk in your EDP-related operations, you should discuss this with the EDP manager. You should expect to clearly define areas that you believe require improvement by the EDP department and specify what improvements you believe are required by personnel under your direction. The improvements may cost money (staff time or real dollars) and you should be prepared to provide the required funding.

5.3 FIVE SUGGESTIONS FOR GETTING YOUR REQUIREMENTS IMPLEMENTED

The actions recommended in this section represent a recent trend by some organizations and managers to place responsibility for assets and resources closer to the ultimate decision-maker. The recommendations will parallel the thinking of those managers who support dispersed data processing. The recommendations may seem controversial to those managers who support a strong centralized data processing department.

The recommendations will apply equally to those managers who are responsible for large application systems development and to those managers responsible for microcomputer applications development. The primary differences will be the number of people who are directly involved, and the level of detail that can be supported by micro applications.

1. Assume a Very Active Role

The best way to get your control requirements implemented is to specify those controls that you require and then audit for compliance by both your staff and the EDP department. This means very active participation by you and your staff in areas that were once the sacred and perhaps sole responsibilities of the EDP department and the auditing department.

2. Participate in Application System Development

You, not the EDP department, should be the absolute authority on what is necessary for a computer application system to meet your operational and control requirements. You may have to make concessions and compromises on operational capabilities and niceties based on costs, management whim, or business realities. However, concessions or compromises on control and security matters should be made only on the basis of risk that you are willing to assume when the consequences of vulnerability exploitation and the costs of the remedies are fully understood.

You, as the responsible manager, are probably the initiator of a request for a new application system. Major revisions of existing application systems are not unlike new application requests and should be handled in a similar manner. The methodology for getting from your "glimmer of an idea" to an implemented system may be specified for your organization or you may have a choice of procedures. Consider this fundamental approach as a practical way to get an application system developed so that it really meets your requirements.

Develop Preliminary Requirements

Earlier in this chapter we discussed reviewing application objectives. The application development process starts with the specification of the objectives that a system must meet. They need not be highly detailed, but they must be sufficiently clear so that those people who will be involved—your staff and the EDP department staff—know what you want.

The preliminary requirements should include all of the major functions that the system is to perform, the outputs (reports, actions, and such) to be provided from the system, and the inputs to the system (forms, phone orders, and such). It is more important at this point to give an overall view than to discuss any particular area of concern in great detail.

The requirements should include those from other departments of the organization that would be involved in or be impacted by the system. The other departments may have additional or different control needs that must be incorporated into systems design criteria during the early planning stages. This is especially important if they will have approval or disapproval of the final design of the system.

Laws, regulations, and company policies that will impact the proposed system should be included as part of the preliminary requirements. This may involve input from the auditing and legal departments. Systems that will contain people-related data (customer as well as employee), and systems that involve the passing of data across national borders require special attention to legal concerns relating to the privacy and confidentiality of personal information.

Review System Availabilities

There has been a growing trend to purchase generalized computer application systems rather than to develop them in-house. Two major advantages of this approach are quicker implementation time and a reduced need to hire long-term staff members for system development and maintenance.

Prospective system vendors should be advised of your intention to use their services as part of your requirements definition for a possible later bid. One drawback of this approach is dealing with overly zealous sales representatives. You must be able to firmly communicate your initial needs as only informational or you may find some vendors to be more of an aggravation than a benefit.

Prepare Detailed Specifications

You will need to prepare detailed specifications of your system's objectives and functions, as well as its operational and control requirements. You may be considering purchasing an application system, or you may anticipate in-house development. The procedure for developing specifications is the same.

Developing the detailed specifications will require some technical expertise. You may have trained staff members or you may require assistance from the EDP and EDP auditing departments. The American Management Associations provide an excellent course on specifications preparation. If your staff has never prepared specifications, this course would be most helpful.

There are conventional methods to acquire an application system: purchase a previously written system, have the system built by in-house staff (EDP's or your own), or contract with a software vendor for a custom-built system. Your organization's policies, staff resources, cost, and timing considerations may constrain your available options.

Test the System Before Acceptance

You, as the person responsible for the application system, must thoroughly evaluate the results of all system testing prior to allowing the system to be placed into production status. The testing to be performed may have been specified as part of the system requirements. More likely, it will be developed during the design phase of a custom-built system or be provided as part of an "off-the-shelf" application system.

Be overly cautious in your evaluation of all system testing. Remember, you, not the data processing manager, will be held accountable by your management or the audit department after the system has been accepted.

3. Review Application System Maintenance

You must assume responsibility for reviewing all changes made to application systems after they have been placed into production status. This is part of the integrity controls process. It is the only way that you can be certain the application controls remain intact.

An application system becomes eligible for maintenance as soon as the user accepts it and the system is placed into production status. Systems that remain in test status for prolonged periods of time are unacceptable exceptions to this general concept.

An application that lingers in test status may be an indicator of a system in difficulty or it may be an indicator of inadequate documentation for the application to be turned over to the operations staff. Either reason should be cause for concern on your part.

Normally, two types of changes are made as part of the maintenance— changes due to new requirements and changes made to fix bugs.

New Requirement Changes

All requests for application system changes should be initiated by you or your staff. Requests must be in writing and specify the reason for the change and the application system changes to be made.

Common reasons for new requirement changes include:

- changed processing procedures requirements
- change in legislation, regulations, rules
- additional information requirement
- modified information requirement
- operating system change
- equipment change
- expansion of the system to accommodate more users.

Changes to Fix Bugs

It is not uncommon for application programs to fail after they have been in production status for some time. The reasons are usually attributable to previously untested application conditions. Sometimes programmers refer to these as bugs. Often, the problems may be related to bad data or a data condition that was not anticipated by the system designer.

Program changes to fix bugs may not be initiated by you. They may be changed in the night by a programmer to meet the application's production deadline. Your control concern should be how and when you become informed.

Your ability to control the maintenance changes to your application system will depend heavily on the operations controls present in the EDP department. They are discussed in more detail below. At this point you should know the answers to these questions:

A. How are your programs protected from all unauthorized access?

B. How do you become aware of all changes that have been made to your application systems?

C. How do you know that only those changes which were authorized were made?

D. How well, and for how long, is the documentation of the changes maintained?

4. Review Operating System Maintenance Controls

Operating system programs directly control the environment in which your application system programs are executed. Most operating system changes will not affect how your application programs are executed. However, some maintenance changes to the operating system may have an effect on the specific functions of your appplication system's operation.

ZAP programs are special utility computer programs that are needed to maintain operating system software. They can also be used to repair damaged data. ZAP programs are designed to enable the user to look at or make changes to data or programs without leaving an audit trail. Be sure that you are comfortable with how the use of these programs is controlled. (See SUPERZAP, in Chapter Nine.) The practical extent of your review of operating system maintenance may be limited to the controls exercised to restrict the use of the ZAP programs which are commonly used to make operating system changes.

5. Review Operation's Controls Effectiveness

The computer operations department may have complete custodial responsibility for your data and programs. You must review them or trust the competency and thoroughness of your organization's audit department. Consider asking the head of computer operations the following questions:

How Can Your Data Be Accessed?

This is a very broad question. Let's look at the possible pieces that can make up the answer. The first restriction in place should be logical access control software (Chapter Two) that limits access ability to specific personnel, programs, and devices. If logical access control software is not in use, the answer from operations may be that anyone can access your data.

Physical access control should not be overlooked. Your data may be valuable enough for someone to physically steal a tape to copy it.

Backup tape protection should also be discussed at this time. It would be reasonable to assume that you have multiple copies of your data for the purpose of restoring lost or damaged data. You must determine if this data has the same degree of protection as the data that you normally use, because it may be easier to breach the confidentiality of your information by getting to your backup data, than from data currently in production status.

Who Can Access Your Data?

It would be comforting to believe that only you or your staff decide who could gain access to your secured data. However, even in a very well-controlled data center it would be reasonable to assume that computer security officers, EDP auditors, and systems programmers may have the technical ability, and perhaps management authorization, to look at or to change your data.

You need to know who can access your data, and under what circumstances.

Who Is Advised of Access to Your Data?

Your computer probably has the ability to log all accesses to your data. Most large computer systems have this capability.

You must determine if the data logging capability has been activated; if reports relevant to your accessed data are prepared; and how a report of authorized and unauthorized accesses is communicated to you.

The data access reports you should be asking for should include all of your data: secured/unsecured, production, and test data. It should indicate the application, the person, when the access occurred, and the device or locations that initiated the access. A practical alternative to reduce the size of this report would be to request an exception report of all accesses except those which you specifically authorized.

Which of Your Application Programs Are Executed and When?

Your production programs are presumably run during certain times of the day, week, month, or year. They are authorized to access your data. You want to know either when they are executed, or, on an exception basis, when they are executed when they shouldn't be executed.

Unscheduled, or multiple program execution, may be an indicator of either a program failure or an unauthorized activity. Both of these conditions should require an explanation to you.

Which of Your Application Programs Are Not Executed?

Request a report of all of your programs that have not been used during the past month. Application programs that are not executed are a vulnerability to you because they are authorized to access your data. Examine the unexecuted program documentation to find out why they are not in use and take appropriate actions.

Which of Your Data Is Not Accessed?

Request a report of all data that is charged to you, tape and disk, and which has not been accessed in the past month. Some of the data that has not been used may have been stored, other data may be on file for backup and recovery purposes. All data that has not been used for more than a month should be explained.

From Which Libraries Are Your Application Programs Executed?

Production status computer programs should only be executed from production libraries, and the production libraries must be maintained under strict operational controls. The production libraries are usually on disks that can only be accessed by a control or a production unit.

It is not uncommon to find production computer programs being executed from test libraries. These bypass operational controls and their continued existence in test status should not be permitted.

Similarly, you may find that some programs are executed from a "pseudo-production" library. This is also undesirable. Two common excuses given for having pseudo-production libraries are to test program maintenance and for one-time use of special programs. Both of these excuses are unacceptable.

Which of Your Application Programs Have Failed During the Past Month?

Request a report of program failures during the past month. You may also want to request a full year failure report. Ask for an explanation of the cause and remedy for each failure.

Additionally, in conjunction with the program failure report, determine what happened to the outputs from the failed programs, especially negotiable documents and sensitive reports.

What Happens to Damaged Negotiable Documents and Sensitive Reports?

Computer printers sometimes damage or destroy negotiable documents or sensitive reports. This can occur after successful program execution while the output is being released to the printer. The program that produced the output does not necessarily have to be rerun. A copy of the output data is merely re-released to the printer.

You must determine whether damaged sensitive documents should be destroyed or returned to your staff for destruction. The presence of a shredder in a computer room does not necessarily ensure the destruction of your damaged printouts.

How Is the Continuity of Your Data Processing Protected?

You cannot assume that your computer center will always be available to process your data and to support your operational requirements. You must be certain that adequate procedures and facilities are in place to protect your applications processing continuity, or that you have fallback procedures and resources to cope with a reasonable period of processing outage; perhaps you may need both.

Here are some of the indicators of a properly planned EDP disruption contingency plan:

- Proper backup vaulting procedures. Computer programs should schedule backup copies of your data and programs on a schedule that has been defined by your staff. The physical backup copies should be moved to the off-site storage facility on a schedule that reflects your recovery requirements.

- Adequate separation of the off-site data and program storage facility. Look for a storage facility removed from the computer room. A location several miles away from the computer room would be better than one in a nearby building.

- The computer room, tape library, and off-site storage vault should have fire and intrusion detection and response equipment. Video equipment wired to a security location would be a plus.

- Regular audits of library contents are performed by the operation department. A weekly physical match of what is supposed to be in the off-site storage facility to what is actually there should be performed by the computer operations staff.

chapter 6
How to Deal with EDP Auditors

This chapter describes what the auditee may expect from the auditor. It suggests methods for surviving an audit, as well as for getting the maximum benefit from the EDP audit department.

Look for ways to improve your relationship with the EDP audit department as you read this chapter. Don't expect to find a secret method to develop a cordial relationship with your auditors. Do expect to receive realistic audits that focus on material control weaknesses that provide management with the opportunity to accept documented and reasonable business risks.

6.1 UNDERSTANDING THE EDP AUDITOR'S MISSION

The mission of the EDP audit department is to provide the organization's management with a reasonable degree of assurance that the organization's controls are in compliance with appropriate laws, regulations, policies, and procedures. The EDP audit department may also be charged with the responsibility for evaluating whether EDP management is efficiently using the resources entrusted to it, and with conducting investigations in situations where fraud or negligence has resulted in lost assets.

The EDP audit department meets its mission by evaluating the effectiveness and controls adequacy of application systems, systems software, and the operating environment in which the systems and data are used. Some EDP audit departments extend their activities into the design and development of application systems, and the purchase or development of operating system components.

Individual EDP audit managers and auditors must meet the requirements of the audit function in an area where the ground rules are uncertain. Traditional business auditors have a large body of practical experience, precedents, and accounting procedures for guidance in paper ledger-based financial and general business activities.

EDP auditing does not have the benefit of many years of precedents and experiences. It is a new field, bound by traditions of the past that must be modified to cope with the changing technological realities of the present. The period of transition may be painful for you, the audit department, and the organization.

Your dealings with the EDP audit department's manager and individual auditors may range from business cordiality to hostility. It is doubtful that any manager's dealings with any real control function could ever be termed pleasant. You should expect fairness when there is a mutual concern for security and control, and where an atmosphere of realistic cooperation prevails. Here are some suggestions to help you develop an interim strategy for determining what your EDP audit department's true mission may be, and how it may affect you.

1. Develop an Understanding

Determine what the EDP audit department's apparent mission in your area of responsibility appears to be. This understanding must be based on your previous control and security actions, personal relations with the EDP audit department's staff members, and the type of EDP audit manager your organization currently has. The following simplified description of EDP audit managers may be of assistance.

Helpful

An audit department that is properly managed and is staffed by people with a good mix of professional EDP and auditing skills will conduct tough audits. Questionnaires will seem to be on target. Substantive examinations of program documentation will be performed. Independent tests of how programs and program subroutines function will be performed. You and your staff will know that they had a workout.

Helpful auditors may attempt to "break" your security with your prior knowledge and authorization, and perhaps cooperation. Your staff may complain about the excessive time required to answer auditor questions, but there will be few complaints about "the idiots from auditing" asking fundamental questions. (Note: IDIOT is the technician's term for an EDP incompetent.)

Audit reports will note real problem areas. Corrective actions which are initiated during the course of the audit will be clearly indicated. Auditor assistance in developing solutions may be mentioned, but not with the auditors receiving excessive credit for being the prime movers of the corrective actions.

Audit reports may include recommendations for increased staffing and additional hardware and software. Helpful audit managers may include a few comments about the adequacy of your controls in the audit's management highlights letter. Details about minor deficiencies will be included in specific comment areas rather than in the highlights letter.

A NOTE OF WARNING. Some helpful audit managers may be compelled by EDP manager resistance, or by their own inner needs, to breach your security systems without prior authorization to demonstrate a lack of security. This should not be tolerated!

Bean Counter

The safest role for an audit manager to play in some organizations may be that of a bean counter. Bean counters simply enumerate specific problems and make general recommendations. This is very easy to detect by reviewing the past year's audit reports.

An obvious tip-off during the conduct of an audit will be the use of lengthy checkoff questionnaires with vintage forms. The emphasis will be on paperwork maintained to document what you have done and are doing. Few in-depth attempts will be made to test or evaluate automated controls and computerized records; rather, the auditors will request and rely on reports prepared by EDP department staff members.

Another tip-off may be audit staff qualifications and turnover. Incoming EDP auditors may be very bright but lacking in experience. Very few senior level EDP auditors will be recruited; those that are hired will not stay long.

You may receive complaints from your technical staff about excessive time spent answering questions about data processing fundamentals. Your staff may even overhear a few auditor complaints that indicate dismay over not finding any faults to write up.

The audit reports will criticize you for any nontraditional means that you may use to control your operations. They may point out numerous minor deficiencies and weaknesses in the management highlights letter, as well as in the specific audit findings, with little apparent regard to materiality. Rarely will such words of praise as "there appears to be an adequate level of control" appear in a highlights letter.

Recommendations for improvements will be short and generalized with few specific suggestions for improvements. Requests to review your proposals may be frequent but they will get responses akin to audit reports. Auditors will generally avoid spending time on projects that appear to be well planned and controlled, and these projects will not get audit report format reports.

Survivalist

Audit managers who do not have an adequate understanding of data processing, and who also do not have sufficient EDP audit staff resources, may choose to perform limited audits of data processing activities. General questions may be asked, with every effort made to find compliance with whatever is applicable. Little, if any, effort will be made to examine operational or test computer programs.

Audit reports will be generally favorable. Blatantly obvious deficiencies may be noted. Phrases such as "severe deficiencies" or "extreme weaknesses" will rarely appear anywhere in the audit.

Survivalists are a vanishing type of auditor. Their inability to cope with rapidly changing EDP and audit technologies make their unsuitability to the audit profession increasingly obvious to both EDP and general audit management. Modern business management, with limited resources, simply cannot tolerate survivalist EDP auditors or EDP audit management.

2. Confirm Your Understanding

Your perception of the audit department's mission must be confirmed if it is to serve as the basis for your future relations and methods of dealing with EDP auditors. Try some of the following suggestions and evaluate the responses:

- Meet with the highest level audit manager about your next major application or operating system change. The purpose of the meeting will be to determine what EDP auditor help will be made available to you.
- Request a warranted upgrade to the next audit report's management highlights letter.
- Meet with the highest level audit manager to review planned audit projects and individual staff member assignments.
- Request staff turnover reports for the audit department.
- Request the qualifications of each EDP auditor assigned to work in your department, with specific emphasis on the tasks that he is to perform within the audit work plan.

3. Effect a Mission Attitude Adjustment

The mission of the EDP audit department with respect to ensuring the proper utilization of the organization's assets should closely parallel your own. The only acceptable areas of disagreement between you and the audit organization should be how well you are meeting your control objectives, and how the audit department presents its evidence and conclusions that you are, or are not, meeting those objectives.

You can benefit from the assistance of the EDP audit department. It can serve to document your need for additional resources and serve as a conduit for conveying your accomplishments and ideas to upper management. Conversely, the EDP audit department can add to your managerial burden. You have a responsibility and an opportunity to encourage and utilize the services that your organization's EDP audit department can provide. You have an obligation to act accordingly.

6.2 HOW TO SURVIVE AN EDP AUDIT

You will not survive an audit by rolling over and playing dead. You will survive an audit by maintaining a demonstrable level of control that is consistent with the level of risk that system users and the organization's management wishes to assume.

Alan Brill summarized the philosophy of a fair audit as:

> Finally, auditing can be considered as risk evaluation and detection. But the risks should not be the sole concern of data processing. Users are directly and often vitally affected by data processing problems. They should have some say in risk assumption. And since risk management is part of a DP manager's job, an effective program of EDP auditing and of responding to audit findings will turn fear into the recognition that audits, while they will never be fun, can, at least, be used as tools to improve the operation and management of the data processing function.[1]

The fairness with which you are treated in an audit report should be based on a professional assessment of factual audit findings. You have an obligation to present these facts to the auditors during the audit process. Don't expect an auditor to do all the work. Help him every step of the way.

1. Review the Objectives of the Audit Before It Starts

A thorough understanding of the purpose of an audit will save you and the auditors time. It will also give you the opportunity to request a postponement of audits of systems where you expect significant changes to occur.

The auditors should define which systems they plan to examine, and the types of controls that they plan to test. The auditors may plan to examine both integrity and application controls, as well as the operating environment. That will be a tougher audit.

The audit manager should welcome your request for specifics about the proposed audit. Auditors usually budget their time for audit field work. You can save auditor time and save your time by proper preparation.

---

[1]Alan Brill, "Why Data Processing Managers Fear EDP Audits." Reprinted from INFOSYSTEMS, August, 1982, p. 80. Copyright Hitchcock Publishing Company. Used by permission.

Try to obtain as many specifics about the audit from the audit manager as she will impart. The audit manager may be more helpful in providing initial detailed information than the auditor(s) who will be performing the fact gathering. Junior auditors may be especially reluctant or unable to provide substantive preparatory information if this is their first time performing an audit in an unfamiliar area.

2. Request Appropriate Postponements

All audits do not need to start or end at the convenience of the audit department; especially audits performed by the internal audit department. The time to voice valid reasons for a change of schedule is *before* the audit begins. Some valid reasons for delay are:

- planned major system changes;
- planned discontinuance of a system;
- staff working heavy overtime schedule to meet new system implementation date;
- scheduled implementation of new logical access control software.

Some unreasonable reasons for a postponement are:

- too busy with general workload to assign right staff members;
- month-end closing time;
- system in question was just audited.

3. Assign an Audit Coordinator

You, or a manager on your staff, should be assigned the responsibility for coordinating and resolving all auditor requests and conflicts, specifically:

- staff member unavailabilities
- conflicting statements of facts
- obtaining computer run time if scheduling becomes a problem
- maintaining audit target or milestone dates
- previewing exit interviews
- reviewing and preparing responses to preliminary draft audit reports

The appropriate manager on your staff should schedule a meeting of staff members and the auditors prior to the start of each audit. This will help to assure that the most knowledgeable staff members will meet with the auditors. The coordinator's role with regard to scheduling is to make certain that all reasonable deadlines are met.

4. Protest All "Fishing Trips"

Staff members should be advised that requests that exceed the stated scope and objectives of an audit are to be immediately reported to their supervisor or the audit coordinator. This will reduce the potential for auditors getting sensitive information without proper authorization. It will also help to reduce the amount of excess time spent by your staff in dealing with matters that are not relevant to a particular audit.

Audit personnel who are conducting fraud-related audits are an exception to this suggestion. Fraud auditors must at times ask seemingly absurd or excessively vague questions to prevent the subject from learning enough about an investigation to compromise it.

5. Review Preliminary Audit Reports

The preliminary audit report provides the last chance to catch errors in an audit report before it goes public. It is important for you and the auditors to be sure that the facts are correct; and the conclusions drawn from the facts must be clearly understood by all concerned. This should be the responsibility of your audit coordinator and the audit manager.

As an example, while serving as an audit coordinator and reviewing an audit report with an auditor and his manager, I noticed a finding and recommendations dealing with unit record equipment that had been removed several months earlier. The audit report was badly behind schedule and the auditor had failed to properly confirm his facts. The auditor's manager was very appreciative. The auditor was somewhat embarrassed. The finding was removed from the audit.

Preliminary audit reports also provide an opportunity to review and discuss audit recommendations and conclusions. Issued audits have to be defended—by both sides. It is much easier to have a give-and-take session before the audit report is issued.

6. Protest Unfair or Incorrect Audits

Unfair or incorrect audits are issued sometimes. These should have been remedied during the exit interview or preliminary audit report review process. Once in a while, however, a goof can occur. Protest loudly when you are backed by the facts.

Rebut the facts and/or conclusions when you are right. Err on the side of conservatism, if you must err at all.

7. Make Improvements Where Warranted

Business managers have a right and an obligation to assume justifiable risks in their areas of responsibility. Data processing managers, however, cannot be permitted to jeopardize the business's managers by not properly securing systems. Unsecured systems distort the risk/ decision process.

Make the reasonable improvements recommended by the auditors, or explain to the business manager why the improvements are not warranted, and let her decide on the course of action to follow. Document all decisions, with special attention to the "no action" items. Recommendations that are simply ignored may be real vulnerabilities to the organization, or they may be lying dormant to become bigger problems when the auditors return for a follow-up visit.

6.3 HOW EDP AUDIT CAN HELP YOU TO IMPROVE SECURITY

EDP auditors can help you to improve the quality and control of your systems development and operations. The extent to which this help will benefit you depends on the qualifications of the EDP auditors in your organization, the audit manager's attitude and philosophy, and your own attitude and philosophy towards the auditors.

The Systems Auditability & Control (SAC) Study[2] conducted a survey in which data processing managers were asked to characterize internal audit involvement in terms of the following four criteria:

---

[2]Systems Auditability & Control Study Audit Practices, Institute of Internal Auditors, 1977, pp. 40–43. Used by permission.

- Causes increased or decreased costs
- Harmful or helpful
- Worthless or valuable
- Unavailable or responsive

The results of the study indicate that internal audit involvement is viewed as both helpful and valuable. It is more often characterized as responsive than not. In terms of costs, slightly more than one-half of the data processing representatives feel that auditing neither increases nor decreases costs; the remainder are about evenly split between those who believe that internal auditors decrease costs and those who indicate that internal auditors increase costs.

Finally, data processing managers were asked to identify two ways that data processing has benefited most from the efforts of internal audit. The three most frequently checked areas of benefit were improved application system controls, reduced fraud/loss exposure, and increased user confidence and satisfaction. Interestingly, however, almost one-third of data processing managers believe that no significant benefits have resulted from internal auditors' efforts.

The SAC Study classified application system audit involvement in six categories:

Development Requirements

Developing Functional Specifications

Establishing Testing Procedures

Monitoring Data Integrity During Implementation

Postinstallation Review

Periodic Application Reviews

These classifications would apply, in part, to both new application systems and existing application systems. The data processing manager who requests audit's assistance will not have the ability to control, or to accept or reject with impunity, any recommendations made by the auditors. Therefore, it is necessary to have an established good working relationship before requesting assistance from EDP audit.

Some EDP audit departments extend their activities into operating system and network control system reviews. This level of assistance requires that the audit department have substantial systems programming and data communication skills. It is an area that will receive more auditor attention in the future, as more skilled auditors become available.

chapter 7
Improving Productivity
As a Security Byproduct

This chapter discusses operational problems that can be reduced by improving security. It identifies specific sources of errors and recommends a course of action for making improvements.

Use the suggestions presented in this chapter to identify those computer applications that should be modified or replaced to effect both savings and security improvements. Also use the suggestions as a basis to help managers get past the "if it's not broken, don't fix it" syndrome that can result in technological stagnation for the organization.

7.1 HOW TO IDENTIFY COMPUTER-RELATED PRODUCTIVITY PROBLEMS

Improving computer security can improve the productivity of your operations. Do you find that hard to believe? It shouldn't be if the thrust of your computer security program is getting people the information that they need; making sure that the information is correct, timely and complete; and keeping unauthorized people from getting information that could result in harm to the organization.

This chapter will help you identify and resolve problems that reduce computer-related productivity. Some of the problems are security related. Some aren't. However, it is not uncommon to detect and remedy operational problems in the course of conducting a security review. So, yes, improving security can improve productivity.

Computers improve productivity by either doing work better or faster than it is now being performed or by helping people to perform the work that they are doing better or faster. Computers do not have magic powers. Computers are tools that need to be used effectively to improve productivity.

Consider a somewhat arbitrary distinction needed to deal with computer-related productivity. Classify your business functions as OPERATIONAL and PLANNING, which also includes analysis.

7.1.1 Operational Problems

Operational activities are the "get-the-work-done" functions. They can be measured very precisely in environments where physical units are produced. As an example, a fully automated machine could be programmed to assemble printed circuit boards at the rate of ten per minute. Management could very easily determine if that rate were being achieved. It might then be possible to improve productivity by increasing the speed of the machine and its feeder systems, or by redesigning the board to speed assembly.

The results of an automated assembly operation can also be subjected to automated quality control procedures which can rapidly and reliably check for defects in the end product before it leaves the factory. If, after increasing assembly line speeds, an increase in product rejections became apparent, it would be a clear signal to management that there is a problem that is impacting productivity.

People-related productivity problems are not as easy to detect and remedy as those in an automated operation. The three factors that are obvious in the productivity measurement of manufacturing operations—TIMING (throughput), ACCURACY, and COMPLETENESS—are masked by the actions and interactions of people and computers. Are these problems identified in your organization in the same manner as manufacturing problems? Here is a quick test to find out if you have computer-related productivity problems.

Look at the symptoms that may become obvious to the work force well before management realizes that a productivity problem exists. Eight typical complaints, which may also serve as explanations for work backlogs, are:

1. The computer was down or otherwise unavailable when needed.

2. The computer response time for each on-line transaction or inquiry was slower than usual.

3. The computer-generated information or reports needed to perform the work were not ready on time and the staff had to wait.

4. The computer's information was not current enough and a manual reconciliation was needed to supplement the report.

5. The information in the report was wrong and had to be corrected.

6. Time was spent performing calculations that could have been made by the computer.

7. Time was spent looking up information that was in the computer but not available.

8. People are using the computer for too many outside activities.

Complaints like those listed above indicate that computer-related productivity problems exist and need attention. You may not know the technical reasons for them or the solutions to them, but they are problems that you can identify and they can be solved.

Here are five fundamental causes of the problems described above:

1. CPU Overload

The central processing unit (CPU) may be overloaded because it isn't large enough to handle the increasing workload of the organization. Be careful when given this explanation by the data processing manager. It may cause you to accept a knee-jerk cureall solution that doesn't address your specific problems.

A second reason for CPU overload may be the size of the computer's main memory. An increasing change to on-line processing applications from batch systems without an increase in main memory can make this a valid concern. On-line applications need more main memory than batch systems to work efficiently.

A third reason that your organization's CPU(s) may be overloaded is because the work mix has not been properly scheduled. Your operations may be having problems because work that could be run at night is being scheduled for prime shift attention.

Finally, CPUs can get mysteriously overloaded because they are doing more than the organization's work. It is a common practice in some data processing departments to process personal work on the organization's computer. Forget the direct security concerns for the moment. They are covered elsewhere in this book. Think only about the productivity impact. Your organization's production work may be contending for prime shift processing cycles with staff members' games, homework, recipes, or private consulting services. You should, at the very least, be able to set priorities as to who uses processing resources and when they are used.

CPU overload is a popular excuse for productivity problems. Sometimes it is valid, and more equipment is needed. Sometimes, however, productivity problems related to CPU overload can be solved by better management of the CPU.

2. System Overload

Computer application systems are normally designed to process a known or estimated volume of transactions. Business changes that have occurred since the system was designed may have resulted in processing requirements that exceed the capacity of the current system. Overloaded on-line systems suffer from transactional delays. Overloaded batch systems take longer to process but do not necessarily have a noticeable impact on the user.

3. Network Overload

On-line systems, particularly those that involve extensive data communication networks, can be subject to transactional delays because the network is overloaded. This may be the result of changed or added business requirements; or, it may be the result of a poorly designed network.

It may not be easy to find out if you have a network overload problem. It may require close cooperation between the data processing department and a separate communications department. Hold your data processing manager accountable for proving or disproving network overload as a source of poor transaction response time that impacts your productivity.

4. System Design Maintenance Problems

The older the application system is that you are using, the more likely it is that you are going to have problems with it. This is not because it deteriorates with age; rather, it is because the probability that the system has been changed (maintained) by more people increases with its age, and changes can alter the design of the system.

Typically, application systems grow with changes in business requirements and to add functions that were not previously needed. Sometimes they are changed to correct original design errors.

Each change to an application system adds new ideas. Each new idea that fits within the overall system design framework may not impact your operations. But the totality of new ideas over an extended period of time can put even a patchwork quilt to shame, and it's worse with computer systems.

5. Not-My-Data

The not-my-data syndrome may have invaded your operations. The results can be losses in productivity, security problems, and more than a few sleepless nights.

Not-my-data thrives when explicit ownership and control of data ceases to exist. It impacts your productivity when you must rely on data that others share with you. One symptom is an inconsistency between what you and your staff know should be correct and what isn't correct. Another symptom is that anyone can get any data; it may appear when data leaks occur with some regularity. A third symptom is lost, damaged, or missing data.

Not-my-data problems are solved by establishing data ownership. Once data ownership is established, responsibility for it can be fixed and remedies can be initiated.

7.1.2 Planning and Analysis Problems

Planning and analysis functions of an organization can also improve productivity by improving security, but it may be a tough battle because of changing microcomputer technology and end user programming. Simply put, planners are going to demand that operating units make their data available for processing on microcomputers; and they are going to get the data they need. It's already happening!

The security issues involved in microcomputer processing of data are covered in Chapter Twelve. They include the lack of end user knowledge of security and control procedures, easy loss, damage, or disclosure of data, and the loss of central control over data.

The first productivity impact will be providing the hardware and software needed to get data and programs to and from the micros (and minicomputers) and the mainframes. It's available now. You, or somebody else in the organization, must stay current with technology to keep pace with needs and product availabilities. It will be a difficult task because the demand for skilled technicians will continue to outpace the number of people available.

The second productivity impact will be keeping the end users apprised of the data files that are available. This will result in the need to end the not-my-data syndrome. It will force those organizations that want access to all data to create a central data administration function.

So much for the negatives; let's look at the positives. The planners are going to find that there are numerous redundant data files in organizations with older applications portfolios, and that it is hard to access these multiple files. They will then find some very good economic reasons to, at least, redesign the operating information systems that produce the planning data they need. That can mean real support for the aggressive data processing manager.

The planners are also going to find that the redundant data files don't necessarily agree with each other. As their productivity and abilities are impacted by data problems, they are going to demand and get changes. New York City's pre-crunch financial systems in the 1970s were a prime example of both planning and operational nightmares that were resolved after a crisis.

Two separate city agencies administered most of the city's revenue and expense budget. One was the Budget Bureau and the other was the Comptroller's Office. Each agency had its own information system which was used to control where money came from, how it got spent, and to control and plan for the operating and capital budgets.

The data in the systems did not necessarily agree. Each agency maintained that its data was correct. An army of clerks was needed to resolve the differences. The city could not effectively plan for financial solvency. The answer was new leadership and a multimillion-dollar integrated financial and control system that could provide operational and planning support.

A new city agency was created to build and maintain the one financial system. Productivity was one concern; control and reliability were also key factors. The result was a system that could be used for both planning and operational purposes. Unfortunately, the system became so large that developing the EDP disruption recovery contingency plan—a later consideration—was a major security project.

7.2 HOW TO IDENTIFY AND REDUCE COMPUTER-RELATED ERRORS

Error reduction is different from error prevention. Error reduction is decreasing the frequency or severity of those mistakes, including omissions, that were not prevented. Reducing an error rate requires identifying the source of the errors; and initiating effective corrective actions.

You may choose to assign responsibility for error control or reduction to a separate quality control unit, or you may integrate it within the operations of the business. Does, or should, error control fall within the scope of responsibilities of your computer security officer? It is a logical position to assume error control responsibilities where the computer security officer is part of business operations.

Here is a three-step approach to reducing errors:

1. Identify specific errors.
2. Understand why error rates increase.
3. Develop a well-ordered corrective action plan.

7.2.1 Identifying Specific Errors

This section will help you to identify errors, which are defined to include omissions, that result from intentional or unintentional staff actions. Errors may also be introduced by malfunctioning or poor quality data processing and communications equipment, and these sources of errors will be discussed as equipment-induced errors.

Specific sources of errors have been grouped to follow the flow of data through the processing cycle as follows:

1. data capture
2. data entry
3. programs
4. processing operations
5. error correction
6. equipment-induced

1. Data Capture

Data, in the computer processing sense, usually represents an asset value. If the data is erroneous or absent, the inventory value of the asset will be reduced or overstated.

The asset being represented by the data may be such that if the data is incorrect, it may be corrected and the asset not lost. On the other hand, the asset may no longer be available to be reexamined and revenue will be totally lost if not captured on the first try.

Data capture is distinctly different from data entry where batch processing techniques are used. Data capture is synonymous with data entry for some on-line applications. Consider as an example a major revenue application for large municipalities—parking tickets.

Parking ticket issuance has been by batch application where the data is available on a one-time-only basis. The ticketing agent cannot go back and correct an error. The data must be captured correctly or it gets away, and revenue may be lost if the person receiving the ticket does not remit the fine.

A note about parking tickets: Many people simply send the ticket and a check to the collection agency. However, many other people simply ignore tickets. During the early 1980s, cities like Boston and New York City had many millions of dollars in uncollected parking ticket revenue and they began aggressive programs to collect ticket fines. Correct license plate data became necessary to the collection process.

The data entry form is the parking ticket. The ticketing agent copies the vehicle's license plate number, agent number, vehicle description, and event description onto the form. One copy of the form (ticket) is left on the vehicle. The second copy is used for data entry at a later time.

The cause of any error in the data capture process of the parking ticket application, assuming that the license plate had not been stolen, would be an uncorrectable human error. If the license plate number was incorrectly copied or omitted, and if the vehicle's owner noticed this error, the ticket could be ignored, and an easily quantifiable revenue loss could be measured.

The parking ticket example should be contrasted with another familiar batch application—utility meter readings. Meter reading errors are harder to make and can be corrected at a later time without a significant potential loss of revenue.

The meter reader can be provided with a data entry form or other recording device which has the meter number and address of the meter's location. The meter's display is recorded, and this value is later input to the computer by a data entry operator, a document reader, or other specialized equipment.

The extent of any potential revenue loss from this data capture operation is very limited. If the recorded meter value is too low, the error may be detected during the computer processing cycle, and the same or another meter reader dispatched to capture the data again. A more practical way of correcting the error is to compensate for it during the next reading.

The specific causes of errors for other business data capture applications can be similarly defined. They are related to individual events, and the revenue losses that may result from intentional or unintentional errors and omissions of any one person can be limited to the incorrect activities of that one person. One significant exception, however, is the loss of an entire batch of documents, or the failure to have a sufficient number of data collection forms available. (The City of Cleveland ran out of parking ticket forms in 1984, and ticket revenues declined sharply.)

2. Data Entry

Batch Systems

The data entry process in batch applications, like those which were described above, follows data capture. The data on the data entry forms is input to the computer system by people using data entry devices or directly by machines such as document readers.

Data entry operators process the consolidated work of many other people. Errors may be introduced during the data entry process that go beyond the activities of any one individual. One person or machine can make intentional or unintentional errors that can impact the quality of many other employees' work.

Here we begin to see the potential errors that may be caused by the equipment itself. However, let's look at the human error potential, and the controls that should normally be in effect. Equipment-induced errors will be discussed later.

Data entry forms, which are also known as input documents, are submitted to terminal operators in groupings that are referred to as batches. The batches may contain an arbitrary number of items, or items may be processed individually as they are received.

Financial data batches such as receivables may also be accompanied by a control total(s). The control total may be the sum of the payment dollars in the batch and the number of items in the batch.

The terminal operator keys all or selected data fields, such as account number, payment amount, and date of payment. The data entry equipment, depending on the equipment, edits each field (see Chapter Two) and accumulates a total for the batch. This total, at the end of the entry of each batch, is compared to the previously prepared batch total. Entry of all items in the batch is assumed to be in control if the totals match. Otherwise, the source of the error must be determined.

Some data entry operations require that the data be keyed a second time by a different operator to be sure that it has been keyed correctly. This procedure is defined as VERIFICATION. The verifier operator is responsible for detecting and correcting errors that were made during the data entry process.

Data that is keyed and verified should have very few errors that result from the input process. It has been checked by two people and the input equipment. However, (1) the data which has been input cannot be better than the data which has been captured; and (2) errors will get through this process.

Let's look at our parking ticket example again. If the wrong license plate number was entered by the ticketing agent, it could not be corrected by the input operator, the verifier, or the equipment, and revenue would still be uncollectable.

Errors that are made during the input process, once detected, can be corrected by reference to the source documents. They do not necessarily result in lost revenue if they are detected early enough.

On-line Systems

Data entry for on-line systems can have an advantage over batch systems data entry from the standpoint of error reduction. It permits the computer to:

A. Verify that a valid account number is being credited or debited while the input document is in the possession of the input clerk. The computer performs this function by matching the input account number to the master file of existing, active account numbers.

The input clerk, who may also be the sales clerk or cashier in a complete on-line system, has the opportunity to obtain correct information or stop the sale. If the computer detects an error, input clerks in on-line batch data entry systems have, at a minimum, the opportunity to refer an erroneous item to a supervisor for corrective action after an error has been detected.

B. Perform more extensive edit checks than the data entry equipment can make. This can be effected because the computer system has more data available to it and greater processing power than a data entry terminal.

As an example, point-of-sale terminals which are connected to a computer can use optical scanning equipment to read a product code.

The equipment knows if it read the code incorrectly and can request a reentry. The computer then checks the item number to the master file of item numbers before taking any action. If the number is invalid, perhaps due to some intentional alteration, the computer can request a remedial action.

A clarification about on-line input equipment: Technological changes have made the distinction between input devices that are terminals and computers somewhat fuzzy. Terminals can now be computers with extensive data storage capability. The result is an extremely powerful error prevention capability.

The distinction between error prevention and error detection and correction in on-line systems can be somewhat blurred. Error prevention occurs *before* the transaction has been completed and the data has been accepted by the system. To emphasize again the distinction, error correction occurs *after* the transaction has been completed and the data has been accepted by the system.

A final note: In this section on sources of errors that may be detected and prevented during the input process, no attempt has been made to relate productivity increases to the error detection process. However, they do exist, and are a common reason for developing on-line input systems.

Consider our parking ticket example. Research is being conducted for an on-line system for data capture and input to reduce errors. Ticketing agents would have an on-line terminal to verify that the plate number is valid and corresponds to the make and model of the car to be ticketed. This would reduce errors and increase revenues.

An on-line parking ticket system would also have an important productivity benefit. It could also:

A. Identify the vehicles of scofflaws with multiple unpaid tickets outstanding so that they could be towed away and held for ransom (impounded) until the tickets are paid.

B. Identify stolen vehicles in time for police action.

C. Identify police and official vehicles so that agents don't waste time ticketing them. Silly as it may seem, some ticket agents meet their productivity quotas by ticketing any vehicle at a red-flagged meter.

Control Table Entry

Control tables, such as prices and hourly wage rates, deserve special attention as sources of data entry errors. They may be input in a manner similar to transaction entry; perhaps with fewer controls because only a limited number of personnel are authorized to make these entries.

However, control table entry errors can have a much greater impact on the organization. An incorrect transaction entry may mean a revenue loss for one item. A wrong control table entry, such as a payroll or dividend rate, can result in a much more substantial loss because it would affect many individual items.

3. Programs

Computer programs present the greatest potential for financial and productivity losses that can result from errors, because they process and can modify all of the organization's data.

Programs, and programmers, should be the easiest source of errors to control. The smallest number of people are involved; they are better educated than data entry personnel; and, once a program has been properly tested, it will keep doing the same operation in the same manner without deviation. However, programs and operating systems are changed with some regularity.

Every detected error in a program must be logged. Corrective actions taken to eliminate the error must be similarly logged. Changes that are made to get programs operational in emergency situations may not get the same management review and approval as normal maintenance changes. A formal procedure to deal with emergency situation error corrections is vital to error prevention and reduction as part of program change control.

4. Processing Operations

Errors may be introduced during the computer processing of data that are the result of poor operating procedures or the failure to properly follow adequate operating procedures. They can be very dramatic in highly automated operations because computers process information and print documents very rapidly. Subtle, relatively infrequent, low-impact errors are rarely the result of computer operations problems.

Operational errors may be categorized by the source of the problem or the consequences of the error. Both will be discussed here on the basis of the source of the problem. Following are some examples:

Wrong Execution Procedures

Production computer programs are initiated by people or other computer programs on either a scheduled or request basis. Once the programs are activated, they may run on an ongoing basis for a fixed period of time, or until completed. The period of operation is dependent on the application. Some examples may be helpful. A large airline reservation system may always be in operation; accounts receivable may operate only on weekdays during business hours; payroll may be run in batch mode on a weekly basis.

Specific programs to be executed within an application system, the data to be used as input, and the numbers of reports and destination printers are controlled by procedures. An error in the start-up procedures can result in the following:

- data is destroyed
- resources are misdirected
- application fails to execute
- wrong program is executed
- wrong data is used
- incomplete data is used
- data or reports are misrouted

Properly prepared and maintained execution procedures are necessary to minimize errors. However, errors related to mistakes by operations personnel, which go beyond computerized execution procedures, do occur because the procedures are overridden to meet new or emergency situations, other operational controls are not working, or someone goofs.

Wrong Program Version Executed

Chapter Three discusses the control of source and object programs. The execution procedures only know the name of a program. Operations errors can result when the wrong version of a program is executed. Management controls and the use of source object code maintenance software are essential in a large computer center.

Wrong Data

Job execution procedures reference data by file or by data set name. The file name may or may not include a qualifier for the date created. Errors arise when "yesterday's" data, instead of "today's" data is used. This is an easy error to prevent.

One stock brokerage company that I am familiar with had an embarrassing problem because they used a previous day's trading file. They prepared and mailed duplicate stock trade confirmations for an entire day.

Wrong Forms

Processing execution procedures, manual and computerized, must specify any special forms to be used for printouts. It is then the responsibility of the computer operator to use the correct forms. Normally, using an incorrect form would be immediately apparent at printer setup time and errors could be corrected without substantial delays. However, these errors aren't necessarily caught when obsolete forms are used.

Wrong forms errors also include using paper with too many parts or copies. The result can be disclosure of confidential data. One investigation that I conducted was initiated because a copy of a very sensitive report was found in a trash bin. The execution procedures required three-part (copy) paper. There was four-part paper in the printer. The operator prepared the report on the four-part paper and simply threw the extra copy of the report in the trash bin.

5. Error Correction and Supervisory Actions

Error corrections and supervisory actions can be sources of errors and high dollar losses for any organization. Both may bypass the system controls of the processing application on the assumption that only trusted employees make these changes and, because they are careful, mistakes are not made. This is a fallacious assumption.

Common sense leads us to believe that anyone can make a mistake. Computer crime reports clearly indicate that managers and supervisors have been caught using error correction facilities to embezzle funds. Require effective controls for all error correction activities.

6. Equipment Induced

Data processing and communications equipment can introduce data errors. These errors should be known to your operations department manager because they impact productivity and security. Computers have extensive error detection circuitry. Some errors can be corrected by sending the data through again. The computer retries until it is satisfied or gives up after a predetermined number of failed attempts. These detected errors and retries are logged for corrective actions.

Data communications equipment can be a source of errors. This is a controllable vulnerability if appropriate monitoring equipment is used to detect transmission errors, and transmission equipment is upgraded when necessary. Check with your computer operations and communication managers to see how they log error rates. Check with the appropriate application support managers to see how the processing applications become aware of excessive retry attempts that involve processing or communications equipment.

7.2.2 Why Error Rates Increase

Error rates may increase for distinctly different reasons. Look for these six reasons to help you understand what happened:

1. Error Reporting Changes

An error rate may suddenly increase because someone started counting and reporting errors, perhaps as a result of a management change. This will occur at the start of every new error reduction program and it may startle top management if they have not been informed of the new program.

2. Productivity Improvements

Error detection and prevention controls are sometimes removed from application systems to increase productivity. This may have occurred because someone found what she thought was a better way to get things done and failed to get management approval. It might have been done because an operational level supervisor believed that the controls slowed the work flow when an acceptable product was being produced, and eliminated the "unnecessary" control.

3. Unauthorized Program Changes

Computer programmers are tinkerers; they like to make improvements. Each time an authorized program change is made, they have the opportunity to make minor improvements in other parts of the program. These improvements can include the modification or elimination of controls that didn't work.

Other program changes may have been authorized by data processing management without the business manager's knowledge. A review of the program change log and discussion with the involved programmer(s) is necessary to find out what is really happening in your organization.

4. Staff Reductions

Error reports may not be reviewed and acted upon because staff levels were reduced and the operating unit still had to meet the same workload. Staff level reductions can also lead to unauthorized program changes.

One manager, during an investigation of a revenue system problem, admitted authorizing the removal of program controls to reduce error reports that operating personnel could not cope with. He also stated that other controls were removed because they were undocumented and no one could understand the purpose of keeping them in the system.

5. New System Implementation

The implementation of a new application system may result in a sudden change in an error rate. This may be attributable to poor system design, lack of preimplementation training, or a conversion problem. Also, part of the new system implementation process may include finding and correcting errors that were present in the old system, but which had not been previously detected.

6. Staff Turnover

A gradual increase in an error rate may mean that experienced employees are leaving and that their replacements are not being adequately selected or trained.

7.2.3 Establishing Priorities for Corrective Actions

The final step in your error reduction program will be eliminating the causes of specific errors. This must be done on a priority basis because the impact of some errors will be greater than others, and because the resources spent on reducing errors should not exceed the losses that could result from the errors themselves. Setting priorities for corrective actions may be based on the results of a study which is very similar to the risk assessment strategy discussed in Chapter Eight. You may choose your own sense of the business to set priorities; however, the more formal six-step approach is recommended.

1. Select the Target System(s)

Select the application system or area of activity for error reduction review. You may wish to use previous audit reports, money at risk, complaints received, or criticality of application function as the basis of your decision.

2. Designate a Review Team

Choose the review team carefully. You will need both operations and data processing personnel. You may or may not wish to include EDP auditors on the basis of past working relationships, and auditor availability and qualifications.

3. Define the Error Classifications

The review team must count errors by classifications that are relevant to your operations and the application which is to be reviewed. The six general categories used above—data capture, data entry, programs, processing operations, error correction, and equipment-induced—can be used as a starting basis. Expand them to meet your specific requirements.

4. Collect Error Statistics and Other Information

Collect the error statistics carefully. Look for other information in the process that will help to substantiate whether the problems are a result of control failures, procedural failures, or the absence of controls.

5. Evaluate the Cost Impact

Determine the actual or potential cost of errors for each application system by functional area of responsibility. You may find that the causes of errors can be related to a specific operation, such as data entry; related to an application system or program; or related to other specific factors.

6. Establish Corrective Action Priorities

The results of the error reduction study should pinpoint specific error problems and the associated costs of those problems. Use this information to establish a corrective action priority plan that will justify the expenditure of resources.

7.3 WHEN TO REDESIGN THE SYSTEM

7.3.1 Application System Life Span

The useful life of computer application systems cannot be readily defined. They do not wear out. They can be transferred from one computer hardware system to the next. It would almost appear that computer programs and application systems could last forever.

Unfortunately, computer application systems and programs don't really last forever. They can be maintained and modified for many years. At some point, however, they fail to meet management's requirements, and a redesign must be initiated.

The Social Security Administration (SSA) may hold the record for application system and computer hardware longevity. In 1983, the SSA requested a one-half billion-dollar appropriation to completely redesign and replace its aging application systems and programs, many of which were in the ten- to twenty-year-old category. The SSA also planned to replace its similarly old computer hardware.

The SSA's management had a very simple reason for this very expensive request. The systems were so old, and had been changed so many times, that management had a real concern that the systems would soon simply fail to operate. The entire SSA revenue accounting and check generation process was in jeopardy.

The SSA example of systems that have reached the end of their life span dramatizes the need for some orderly review of system longevity before the panic button is pushed. The responsibility for initiating the review process belongs to management. Suggestions to assist you in establishing criteria for system redesign follow.

7.3.2 Criteria for System Redesign Consideration

1. Security

The adequacy of system security or the adequacy of controls in a system is, or has been, one of the lowest-priority reasons for system redesign. Here are four reasons for considering the security of your systems as the primary reason for redesigning your system:

A. Change in Control Philosophy

Older systems were designed to rely on people controls which interacted with computer controls. This is obvious in any batch system where the computer operator maintains a control log for an application, or where control totals are manually matched between processing runs.

Manual processing controls may have been effective in the 1960s when control clerks were abundant. They are out of touch with the work philosophies and staffing levels of the 1980s.

B. Controls Omission

Application program controls were not an issue in the 1960s and 1970s. Computer analysts and programmers designed and built systems to meet business requirements from a productivity perspective.

The systems analysts of the 1960s were computer programmers. Programmers who were academically trained graduated from computer science programs. Accounting control concepts were not included in their curricula. Programmers who were trained on the job or at specialized trade schools similarly lacked accounting and control theory training.

Systems analysts of the 1970s included former programmers and a variety of academically oriented people. Again, control theory was not a high-priority issue.

EDP auditors did not exist in any large numbers during the 1960s and 1970s to assist in the development of computer systems. The few audits of systems that did take place "audited around the system." Input data was compared with reports that were generated by the system as part of the business process. Therefore, we can only speculate about the presence of controls in an older system.

C. Absence of Documentation

The documentation which is available for older systems may not be very useful from a security practitioner's viewpoint. It may not be very good from an operational perspective either.

Documentation standards, for many companies, were not very rigorous in the 1960s and 1970s. Where they existed, they weren't always followed. Consider documentation from the programmer's point of view. EDP auditors didn't exist to demand documentation, and programming management could not review every change. Why should a programmer, who changed jobs on an average of less than two years, be concerned about recording activities that wouldn't be examined until after he was gone?

I recently asked a data processing manager of a major corporation about the recoverability of older computer applications at that data center. He sighed and said, "Forget it. They are undocumented and they aren't on our formal backup program. They are not recoverable."

Conduct a similar interview in your company with a manager who must rely on older system documentation. If you receive an answer that sounds like, "We only have a copy of the source code," you don't have any real documentation. If you are told, "We only have the object code, but the program doesn't have any bugs in it," you have an even bigger documentation problem.

D. Controls Retrofit Impracticality

It may be too difficult or too costly to add missing controls to an existing system. This is especially true for batch-oriented systems that are comprised of individual computer programs, each of which creates data files that are passed to the next program.

The results of your error reduction study should clarify any doubts that you may have about adding missing controls to your systems. As an example of the problems that you may encounter, let's assume that data entry errors from handwritten forms are found to be a real problem; specifically, for a payroll application where employees and supervisors must handle time cards frequently.

The error reduction team, for our example, recommends that the best solution to eliminate data entry errors is to upgrade the system to on-line batch entry. This would enable the computer system to match the keyed time card number to a master employee file to make certain that valid employee numbers were being entered. This is a good suggestion. However, it can't be implemented because the system can't run in an on-line environment.

So, the team recommends that a check digit be used. The check digit would add one more number to the employee number. This is another good suggestion. However, it also wouldn't be practical to implement because the team found that many existing computer programs would have to be modified to allow for one more number in the employee number field. Your conclusion might be "It's time for a system redesign."

2. System Maintenance Costs

System maintenance costs are a significant part of every data processing budget where older applications predominate. They may be as high as 50 to 70 percent of the budget. You may want to find out what percentage of your budget is attributable to older system maintenance.

There are valid reasons why maintenance costs are so high. System design is a key factor. Older systems were designed to work on computers that had very little main memory. They had to be operationally efficient and the end result was complex code. Complex code is difficult and expensive to maintain.

Similarly, for older systems, maintenance was not necessarily a design criterion. Programming was almost considered an art form. The best programmers got to build the system knowing that they would not be stuck with maintenance responsibilities. Also, standards stressing design for maintenance didn't exist in many organizations.

Ask your programming manager what her biggest maintenance costs and problems are. Compare these with the complaints of the programmers who must perform the maintenance to develop an understanding of what your system maintenance costs are in terms of dollars, and with respect to any estimate of when your programs can no longer be maintained at any cost. That is the point when both productivity and security will be valid reasons for system redesign.

3. Disruption Recovery

Systems should be designed so that they can be operationally recovered and disaster recovered. Operational recovery is effected when program or data problems occur during processing at the usual data center. Disaster recovery requires restoring processing at a different site.

Could each of your systems be restored at an alternate site in a reasonable time period? (Chapter Ten discusses disaster recovery requirements in detail.) System design and maintenance are key factors. Consider each of these factors in evaluating the need for system redesign on the basis of recoverability:

A. Dependence on Staff

Systems that require experienced staff to operate them are a liability if your staff isn't available. The problem is compounded when adequate documentation is not available. Look for the existence of run control sheets or logs to find out if this applies. Also, look at how people who use the system are trained. Could a reasonably intelligent person pick up a manual and make the system work? (Do operating instructions exist for all of your systems?)

B. *Dependence on Specialized Equipment*

Are your systems designed to use equipment that is no longer available or hard to replace? If they are, you have a recovery problem if you must go elsewhere to process.

Dependence on specialized equipment is a real problem for some government applications because specialized translates to obsolete. The Social Security Administration example earlier in this chapter is again amazing. It is hard to believe that that agency could recover if it were to have a major catastrophe.

C. *Interdependence of Systems*

Older batch systems are perhaps easier to recover than some newer systems, because they do not interrelate with other systems. Systems that require the availability of several other systems for disaster recovery are a vulnerability to your operations if the other systems are not deemed critical for recovery. Check with the person responsible for disruption recovery to see which of your systems may cause you problems.

4. Business Realities

The criteria for system redesign consideration listed above were based on a security practitioner's outlook. They may be used to help support the business reasons for redesigning a system. It is doubtful that they would be the sole reasons for building new systems. There is a certain logical value in believing that an existing, operational system, deficient as it may be, is better than venturing into the unknown with a new system.

The business reality reasons for system redesign considerations include:

A. *Top Management Mandate*

Top management may determine that the information needs of the organization are not being met by existing systems, and demand changes. Major equipment vendors hold senior executive conferences for this purpose. Encourage your top management to attend if you think a change is necessary.

B. Business Needs Change

Data processing systems should be created to serve the needs of the business. When they do not adequately meet that need, business managers will effectively demand changes to existing systems or build their own systems. Many data processing managers in the 1960s and 1970s missed that point but were able to control system redesign criteria to meet their own requirements.

C. Technology Changes

Changes to hardware and software (compilers and operating systems) can force system redesign. It becomes economically advantageous to replace equipment as newer hardware becomes cheaper to operate. The new hardware, such as IBM's extended architecture, also offers new capabilities that older systems can't use, and the technicians begin finding reasons for system redesign.

Compilers and operating systems become obsolete when they are no longer vendor supported. Application system maintenance becomes difficult and then approaches impossible (the SSA syndrome). Redesign becomes essential.

Last, technology changes can permit system redesign to better meet the needs of the business at reduced costs. Redesign then becomes inevitable.

chapter 8

Preventing Computer-Related Losses

This chapter focuses on developing cost-effective security improvements to reduce future losses. It recommends using qualitative and quantitative risk assessments to establish priorities in making security improvements.

Use the suggestions presented in this chapter to create a risk assessment program that makes sense for your organization. Develop a review schedule that is based on major changes to an application, changing business needs, fixed time periods, or other criteria that meet the policies and requirements of the organization.

Your sense of business cost and risk realities, not computer technology, should be the basis for evaluating the level of security needed to ensure that your operations are in control and that losses are minimized. Use the managerial and technical skills of your staff to identify the organization's vulnerabilities to losses, the estimated frequency of losses, and to define prudent improvements that would reduce the loss potentials associated with those vulnerabilities. Then, apply your sense of business needs to implement those measures that will be cost-effective, to reduce the organization's exposure to control deficiencies and losses.

8.1 FOCUSING ON LOSS PREVENTION REALITIES

8.1.1 View Security from a Benefit/Performance Perspective

The benefit of security is the reduction in future losses. Effective computer security programs must focus on "closing the barn door" before losses occur.

Robert V. Jacobson, a noted security consultant, suggested this simple explanation and example.[1]

> Benefit, from a loss prevention perspective, allows the manager to focus on security improvements in relation to the cost of making those improvements. PERFORMANCE then becomes the means to define what the improvement does to effect the benefit.
>
> For example, the *performance* of an uninterruptible power supply (UPS) could be described as reducing the occurrence rate of electric power failures from two per year to one every five years. The *benefit* of a UPS is a reduction in delay losses to users from EDP service outages caused by electric power disturbances and failures.
>
> Here is a realistic example. Assume that you have been asked to act on the following briefly state proposal:

> ### Capital Budget Proposal #1
>
> Install a UPS:
> Cost: Acquisition: $500,000
>   Annual operation: $37,000
>   Present cost (five-year life): $633,000
>
> Performance: Will reduce the occurrence rate of
>   electric power failures from two per
>   year to one every five years

> Note: Present Cost means the total amount of money that one would have to set aside today—i.e., at the present time—to implement the security measure; in this case $500,000 for acquisition plus a $133,000 sinking fund earning twelve percent interest to cover the five-year operating cost of $185,000. (The salvage value of UPS at the end of the five-year life, which would reduce the present cost a bit, has been ignored.)

---

[1]An Introduction to IST/RAMP, International Security Technology, Inc., N.Y., N.Y., 1983. Used with permission.

What is your decision regarding the UPS? Should you approve the expenditure? You probably feel that something is missing from the proposal. You are right! There is no way that you can determine from the proposal if the performance of the UPS justifies its *cost*. You need more information; specifically, what will be the payback of the UPS? Now consider a second proposal:

<u>Capital Budget Proposal #2</u>

<u>Install a UPS:</u>

Cost: Acquisition: $500,000
        Annual operation: $37,000
        Present cost (five-year life): $633,000

Benefit: Will reduce losses to the XYZ system caused by electric power failures at an expected rate of $75,000 per year
          Present cash value (five-year life): $270,000

> Receiving five payments of $75,000 per year, a total of $375,000, is the same as having $270,000 right now (present cash value), and investing it at twelve percent.

It is obvious that you would turn down this proposal. The present *cost* is more than twice as great as the present value of the *benefit*. However, if the loss reduction were estimated at $275,000 per year instead of $75,000, it would look like a good investment. The present cash value of the loss reduction would be $1.08 million which compares favorably with the present cost of $633,000. The key to evaluating the proposal is the benefit analysis.

The best method to develop a benefit/performance perspective of security is to perform a quantitative risk analysis that relates the benefit which may be derived from a particular security measure to the associated cost of that security measure. Quantitative risk analysis is discussed later in this chapter.

Qualitative risk assessment methodologies provide a less precise method of determining the costs and benefits of a security program. They may include cost/benefit relationships, but do not necessarily reach the level of a full quantitative risk assessment.

8.1.2 Don't Overcommit Resources

Reducing computer-related losses will require the dedication and expenditure of resources—people and money. Keep them in balance.

The cost of adding or maintaining any loss prevention control should not exceed the benefit that results from the control.

The next sections provide qualitative and quantitative methods for developing loss expectancies and costs of adding controls. In a real world, quantifiable benefits must be balanced with the unquantifiable benefits that top management may deem essential for organizational and personal survival. Prevention against "hacker hysteria" provides an example of benefits that are hard to quantify.

The economic damage that an unauthorized user (hacker) of a generally well-controlled computer system can do is relatively small. The intangible damage, the loss of organizational or personal credibility, can be very high. The direct result of this potential for high credibility losses can be the allocation of scarce resources to improve controls in a manner that is not justified by the economic benefits that may be derived.

Keep in mind that committing resources is a responsibility of management, not of a technician. Economic and intangible loss potentials must be presented when making requests for the commitment of resources. Make or expect a decision that makes sense for the organization from an executive perspective which must include both tangible and intangible benefits.

8.1.3 Hold People Accountable

People—employees, vendors, customers, and system attackers—are the most important component of every loss prevention program. You can expect to improve security only if the people whose actions you influence choose to improve security. Motivating and controlling your employees and vendors must become your highest security priority. Accountability becomes the enforcement mechanism that deters and detects security violations, errors, and omissions.

Employees will know an organization's security program is serious when they know that their incorrect or unauthorized actions will be detected and they will be held accountable for those actions. Enforced individual accountability provides an incentive to do the job right the first time, and a reason for not trying to beat the system at any time.

8.2 IDENTIFYING AREAS OF HIGH-LOSS VULNERABILITY

8.2.1 The Purpose of Risk Analysis

The Introduction to IST/RAMP, a risk assessment tool that is discussed later in this chapter, provides the following definitions and examples.[2]

> The *purpose of a risk analysis* is to develop risk exposure information as the basis for management action. There are two basic security management actions available:
>
> 1. *Reduce the exposure* to a threat by reducing its occurrence rate or impact effect.
>
> 2. *Reduce the loss* resulting from the impact of a threat by protecting or dispersing assets subject to loss, or by sharing the loss (insurance).
>
> Here are some illustrative examples of these two actions:
>
> 1. *Reduce the Threat Exposure*:
>
> — Install an Uninterruptible Power Supply (UPS) to reduce the rate of electric power failures.
>
> — Install a password protection system to reduce incorrect and unauthorized access to data and systems.
>
> — Relocate an adjacent spray painting operation to reduce the occurrence rate of fire.
>
> — Move the data center from an earthquake fault zone to reduce the occurrence rate of earthquakes at the data center.
>
> — Install an early warning smoke detection system to reduce the percentage of small fires that develop into major fires.
>
> 2. *Reduce the Loss Potential*:
>
> — Purchase business interruption insurance.
>
> — Maintain a capability of transferring operations to an alternate location to reduce delay losses, i.e., backup.
>
> — Enhance external controls to increase the likelihood of detecting a fraud at a lower loss level.
>
> — Divide the computer room with a fire rated partition to reduce the amount of hardware exposed to damage from a single fire.
>
> — Provide standby manual methods for users to reduce delay losses.

---

[2]An Introduction to IST/RAMP, International Security Technology, Inc., N.Y., N.Y., 1983. Used with permission.

8.2.2 Performing a Qualitative Risk Analysis

Qualitative risk analyses are widely used as audit tools. They are more useful for identifying problems than for developing optimal solutions from a cost benefit perspective. They can, however, be used effectively where their purpose and limitations are understood, and they may include quantitative loss and cost information.

A qualitative approach provides a relatively quick way to identify security deficiencies that can result in losses to the organization. It can be used very effectively to determine the general status of the current security program as part of a security improvement planning program. Consider it as a first step that will help you to understand where you are, keep you ahead of the auditors, and provide a reasonable basis to justify the resources required to perform a quantitative risk analysis.

A qualitative risk analysis should not be the only basis for planning a security improvement program, because it lacks the economic specificity which top management needs before committing substantial resources to big ticket items like disaster contingency plans and major facility improvements. (Note: Basic quantitative methods for disaster contingency plans are presented in Chapter Ten.)

The risk analysis must include operational vulnerabilities within the data center and vulnerabilities within specific application systems. The analysis project may provide an ideal time to initiate a disaster recovery plan project, as much of the data will be interrelated. (See Chapter Ten.)

Here is a three-step approach to qualitative risk analysis that will help you to quickly identify security problems and solutions to those problems:

1. Assign a Project Task Force

The risk analysis should be performed by a task force of individuals who understand data processing vulnerabilities and who can recommend specific improvements to reduce those vulnerabilities. Task force members should be managers or supervisors who are responsible for:

- data center operations
- technical support services
- applications development
- application ownership
- EDP auditing
- EDP and general security
- communications

2. Select Evaluation Criteria

The risk analysis team must develop the specific risk assessment criteria that will be used during the analysis. The criteria must be approved by management and be thoroughly understood by all team members who are conducting the analysis.

The National Bureau of Standards (FIPS Pub. 65, pp. 22-27) presents an excellent definition of application system vulnerabilities. They are applicable to both public and private organizations and should be reviewed and understood by the risk analysis team as part of the evaluation criteria establishment process. They are presented in their entirety later in this chapter.

The National Bureau of Standards (FIPS Pub 65, pp. 8-9) also suggests using DATA INTEGRITY, DATA CONFIDENTIALITY, AND ADP (automatic data processing) AVAILABILITY as evaluation criteria for the analysis. This is based on the rationale that, regardless of the cause, any harm that occurs in automatic data processing manifests itself as a loss to the organization in one of the categories that are defined by NBS as follows: (*Note:* ADP is the federal government's terminology for EDP.)

DATA INTEGRITY – The state that exists when automated data is the same as that in the source documents, or has been correctly computed from source data, and has not been exposed to accidental alteration or destruction. Incomplete data, unauthorized changes or additions to the data, and erroneous source data are all considered violations of data integrity.

DATA CONFIDENTIALITY – The state that exists when data is held in confidence and is protected from unauthorized disclosure. Misuse of data by those authorized to use it for limited purposes only is also considered to be a violation of data confidentiality.

ADP AVAILABILITY – The state that exists when required ADP services can be performed within an acceptable time period, even under adverse circumstances.[3]

The risk analysis team may also want to consider the following loss potential as part of the risk analysis:

PHYSICAL DAMAGE – The specific damage that may be sustained by data processing and communications equipment as the result of natural, intentional, or accidental events. While the direct result of the physical damage may or may not result in the significant loss of data processing availability, it will definitely result in a financial loss to the organization.

ASSET DIVERSION – The intentional or unintentional diversion of the organization's assets may be reflected in the three criteria recommended by the National Bureau of Standards. However, substantial financial losses to the organization may also be sustained as a result of embezzlements or theft of service.[4]

3. Conduct the Analysis

The qualitative risk assessment should be conducted on a project basis with fixed deadlines. Team members must be either separated from their regularly assigned responsibilities for the duration of the assessment period, or the assessment scheduled to permit their participation on a regular part-time basis. Their responsibility will be to identify vulnerabilities and recommend corrective actions. Here are four activities required to get this part of the project completed.

A. Identify Vulnerabilities

The first task is to record each of those vulnerabilities and loss consequences that each team member, and her staff, can identify. The loss consequences may be expressed as high, medium, or low, or they may be expressed in actual dollar amounts. Specific responsibilities for corrective actions may be included with the understanding that

---

[3]Guideline for Automatic Data Processing Risk Analysis, (FIPS PUB. 65), National Bureau of Standards, 8/1/79.

[4]Ibid.

they will be reviewed by the entire team at a later time. Figure 8-1 is a sample worksheet from FIPS Pub. 65, p. 13. The letters "i" and "f" represent estimated impact in dollars and estimated frequency of occurrence, respectively. ALE is the estimated annual loss expectancy. They may be replaced with qualitative measurements such as "high," "medium," "low," "often," "rarely," and the like.

Team members should not be constrained to their area of responsibility. The identification process should similarly not be constrained to problems that may only appear to be solvable by any one group.

Note: Lists of identified vulnerabilities are extremely sensitive documents. They must be protected in accordance with the organization's procedures for handling sensitive documents.

B. Consolidate the Vulnerability Lists

The team leader should consolidate the lists of vulnerabilities into one document. It is not necessary to identify which team member submitted any of the vulnerabilities, although the team leader may want to do so to ensure that all members are actively participating in the project.

C. Categorize the Vulnerabilities

The team leader should distribute the consolidated list to all team members with instructions to assign a corrective action priority category to each identified vulnerability. The use of categories, such as immediate, short-range, long-range, and accepted risk, is recommended because the qualitative technique does not necessarily use a standard fixed loss measure, such as dollar amount of loss, as in the quantitative technique.

The entire team can then meet to review the category assignments. Disagreements will undoubtedly arise. The use of a vote procedure will expedite the process and keep it from bogging down.

D. Recommend an Action Plan in Order of Priorities

The team leader should reorganize each identified vulnerability by category as defined by the team and distribute the new list to each team member. The team members should be instructed to list in order of importance the actions required. A simple one-to-five scale for priorities is adequate.

SYSTEM/APPLICATION Data Files	DATA INTEGRITY		DATA CONFIDENTIALITY	PROCESSING AVAILABILITY			COMMENTS
	Modification	Destruction					
	(i) (f) (ALE)	(i) (f) (ALE)	(i) (f) (ALE)	(i) (f) (ALE)	(i) (f) (ALE)	(i) (f) (ALE)	

Figure 8-1. Risk Analysis Worksheet.

134

The team members should also be instructed to add a recommended unit, such as technical services or specific application program development unit, for reducing or eliminating the vulnerability. Team members may also wish to include recommended solutions at this time.

The entire team must then meet to decide on specific priorities, action responsibilities, and target completion dates. Disagreements may arise. It will be the responsibility of the team leader to resolve these differences, or include the areas of disagreement in the action recommendation.

Preparing the action recommendation will be the responsibility of the team leader. It will be the basis for the management recommendation from the team.

8.2.3 Performing a Quantitative Risk Analysis

A quantitative risk analysis provides the only practical means to evaluate the cost effectiveness of maintaining, improving, or reducing security controls and procedures. It can provide management with the means to evaluate security proposals in a manner that is commonly understood—loss in terms of dollars if a vulnerability is exploited, and the probability of that vulnerability being exploited.

Quantitative risk assessment theory is easy to understand. Defining or selecting a procedure that an organization's management will accept as a valid basis for decisions is more difficult. The National Bureau of Standards (FIPS Pub. 65, pp. 9-12), which is based on the work of Robert H. Courtney, Jr., defines a procedure to calculate the AN-NUAL LOSS EXPOSURE (ALE) of any undesirable event. The ALE is an approximate loss statistic that can be developed on the basis of categorized loss expectancies (expressed in dollars) and frequencies of event occurrences (expressed in time-days and years). It is a commonly accepted measurement, although there is some disagreement on how to calculate it as it applies to data processing systems.

"Technology Assessment: Methods for Measuring the Level of Computer Security"[5] reviewed and evaluated six methodologies, in addi-

---

[5] "Technology Assessment: Methods for Measuring the Level of Computer Security," National Bureau of Standards, Draft 9/81.

tion to FIPS Pub. 65, for conducting risk assessments. One of the methodologies reviewed in the "Technology Assessment" is RAMP, the Risk Analysis and Management Program which has been revised and is marketed commercially as IST/RAMP. IST/RAMP is discussed in this section as an example of one methodology that can be used to implement an automated quantitative risk analysis using annual loss exposure, and to present the rationale for using an automated, rather than a manual, system to conduct a risk analysis.

IST/RAMP considers seven evaluation functions as criteria for conducting the risk analysis. They are:

1. Delay Loss. The expected loss resulting from unscheduled interruptions to the data processing work flow.
2. Physical Damage. The expected loss resulting from the impact of damage threats on physical assets.
3. Fraud via EDP. The expected loss from fraud via the EDP systems.
4. Unauthorized Disclosure of EDP Data. The expected loss from unauthorized disclosure of computerized data (master files).
5. Physical Theft. The expected loss from the physical theft of EDP assets.
6. Master File Back-Up. The expected cost of each of three alternate off-site back-up strategies for master files.
7. Master File Privacy Sensitivity. The relative sensitivity of master files based on the privacy of their contents, the relative size of the files, and the relative frequency of processing.[6]

The risk analysis team defines which of the functions are applicable to objectives of the project. The objectives may be very broad, such as a full risk assessment to reduce losses that would result from an EDP disaster; or the objectives could be limited to a specific disruption factor such as the possible installation of a UPS system.

Data collection forms are prepared after the scope of the project has been defined. The forms facilitate the collection and subsequent input of what may be voluminous amounts of data.

Data is input to the system that performs completeness and reasonableness tests. The system then prepares preliminary evaluation reports for team review and, where necessary, data reevaluation and

[6]An Introduction to IST/RAMP, International Security Technology, Inc., N.Y., N.Y., 1983. Used with permission.

refinement. When the risk analysis reports have been accepted by the team as the "best available estimate of future losses," the team can begin to identify and evaluate the loss reduction benefits of various security measures.

The end product of the iterative analysis of security measures/loss reduction benefits is a report of optimized control improvements which can be used to develop a prioritized action plan for management approval. Sample reports are shown in figures 8-2 and 8-3.

Figure 8-2 (IST, p. 23) presents an annualized loss expectancy (ALE) from eight specific threats. The expected damage (EXP/DAM) is based on the actual loss that could be sustained and the probability of the loss occurring. Percent (PCNT) is percent of the total annualized loss expectancy of $26,761. The cumulative (CUMM) percent is the sum of all preceding loss percentages. Figure 8-3 (IST, p. 24) presents the single occurrence loss potential for each of the events in figure 8-2, and relates them to the percent of annual revenue of the organization.

It becomes apparent from figures 8-2 and 8-3 that, for the identified physical damage threats, earthquakes and minor fires represent ninety-two percent of the loss potential at the facility in question. Management at that facility can now make a realistic decision about

NOVEMBER 9, 1984   2:46 PM   PAGE NO.   23
CALCULATE PHYSICAL DAMAGE USING TDBWORK AND ROBWORK.

ANNUALIZED LOSS EXPECTANCY (ALE): DAMAGE THREATS (DOLLARS/YEAR)

NUM.	THREAT NAME	EXP.DAM $ S	PCNT.	CUMM.
42	MINOR EARTHQUAKE MM = 7	$13,928	52.04	52.04
43	MODERATE EARTHQUAKE MM = 8	$5,675	21.21	73.25
20	MINOR COMPUTER ROOM FIRE	$5,122	19.14	92.39
40	RIVER OR TIDAL FLOODING	$624	2.33	94.72
15	PLUMBING FLOODING/ROOF LEAK	$546	2.04	96.76
21	COMPUTER ROOM BURN-OUT FIRE	$399	1.49	98.25
41	HURRICANE OR WINDSTORM	$346	1.29	99.55
45	TORNADO AT D.P. FACILITY	$121	0.45	100.00
	TOTAL	$26,761		

Figure 8-2.

NOVEMBER 9, 1984 2:46 PM   PAGE NO. 24
CALCULATE PHYSICAL DAMAGE USING TDBWORK AND ROBWORK.

SINGLE OCCURRENCE LOSS: DAMAGE THREATS (DOLLARS PER
OCCURRENCE)

(ANNUAL REVENUE $57,500,000)

NUM.	THREAT NAME	DAM. $/OCC.	% ANN.REV.
43	MODERATE EARTHQUAKE MM = 8	$2,837,366	4.935
42	MINOR EARTHQUAKE M = 7	$1,392,702	2.422
21	COMPUTER ROOM BURN-OUT FIRE	$798,648	1.389
45	TORNADO AT D.P. FACILITY	$242,842	0.422
20	MINOR COMPUTER ROOM FIRE	$102,446	0.178
15	PLUMBING FLOODING/ROOF LEAK	$54,619	0.095
41	HURRICANE OR WINDSTORM	$34,600	0.060
40	RIVER OR TIDAL FLOODING	$15,600	0.027

Figure 8-3.

how much funding it is willing to expend to reduce those loss
potentials.

The risk assessment procedure described above could be performed
manually. (Many companies do this process in conjunction with EDP
disaster recovery contingency planning.) However, the manual process
becomes an enormous task when many functions and control alternatives are to be considered.

The benefits which result from the use of an automated risk analysis
system can be summarized as:
1. Results are quantitatively expressed in dollars using a procedure
which has been accepted in advance by management.
2. Information necessary to perform the risk analysis is retained in
computerized files which can be used for future analysis.
3. Various threat scenarios and security measure changes can be
evaluated to identify optimum strategies.
4. Overall costs are substantially reduced because the voluminous
calculations necessary for optimization are performed by a computer.
5. Report preparation costs are substantially reduced because little
manual intervention is required.[7]

---

[7]An Introduction to IST/RAMP, International Security Technology, Inc., N.Y.,
N.Y., 1983. Used with permission.

8.3 REDUCING YOUR VULNERABILITY TO LOSSES

8.3.1 Act on the Risk Analysis Recommendations

The risk analysis results and recommendations should be the basis for your priority list of immediate actions to reduce security vulnerabilities and their associated potential losses. It should also provide a clear indication of management issues that will require your attention to ensure the long-range effectiveness of the organization's computer security program; these may include:

- security policy adequacy
- standards and procedures adequacy
- responsibility definitions
- systems design and maintenance criteria
- auditability and follow-up requirements

8.3.2 Review and Revise Your Security Policy

Review and revise the organization's computer security policy.

A strong, clear computer security policy is a critical factor for improving the organization's security program and reducing loss potential. It must be issued by top management to set directions for the business managers who will have the direct responsibility for ensuring that the organization's financial, data, and processing resources are adequately protected. The policy must:

A. Specify responsibilities such as:

USER MANAGEMENT. The business manager responsible for an operation is responsible for computer assistance to that operation. As an example, the payroll manager is responsible for having employees receive accurate payroll checks even though he may not prepare or distribute the checks. The responsibility includes data collection and storage; processing accuracy, completeness, integrity, and timeliness; the protection of payroll data from intentional or accidental damage, disclosure, or destruction; and ensuring that adequate plans and procedures are in effect to permit processing of critical payroll applications in event of a data processing disaster.

DATA PROCESSING MANAGEMENT. The data processing manager is responsible for implementing the specific application controls requested by the user in the user's computer programs as well as ensuring that the integrity controls in the data center are adequate to protect the application controls. This responsibility includes the care and custody of the users' data and programs, the protection of processing resources, and maintenance of plans and procedures to permit critical applications processing at alternate locations if that becomes necessary.

EDP SECURITY MANAGEMENT. The EDP security manager is responsible for providing guidance on policy and technological matters relating to data security, data center security, and disaster recovery contingency planning. This responsibility extends to the identification of potential loss factors, recommendations to prevent those losses, and the detection and investigation of incidents where losses have occurred. Organizational positioning of the EDP security management function should also be considered as a policy issue. The Federal General Accounting Office recommends that, "to be effective the information security function must be organizationally located so that it functions independently of line management and reports directly to senior management."[8] This is as relevant to private industry as it is to the federal government.

EDP AUDIT MANAGEMENT. The EDP audit manager is responsible for reporting compliance with management policies, standards, and procedures, as well as for providing guidance on the development of those policies, standards, and procedures. This responsibility should extend to assistance to both user and data processing management in the timely development of cost-effective controls to prevent losses, rather than providing an after-the-fact evaluation of controls omissions.

OTHER STAFF MANAGEMENT. Other staff management members, such as legal, human resources, and so forth, must

---

[8] "Federal Information Systems Remain Highly Vulnerable to Fraudulent, Wasteful, Abusive, and Illegal Practices," U.S. General Accounting Office (MASAD - 82 - 18), April 21, 1982, p. 28.

be held responsible for their areas of expertise and service.

VENDORS. Vendors to the organization must be subject to the same responsibilities for protecting the assets of the organization as employees of the organization.

B. Specify what is to be protected, such as:

DATA. Assign responsibilities for data collection, use, disclosure, storage, and retention.

COMPUTER PROGRAMS. Assign responsibilities for development, testing, maintenance, operation, and disclosure (preferably nondisclosure).

PROCESSING RESOURCES. Define what processing resources may be used for, and who may use them. Encourage the controlled use of the organization's computers for the advancement of employee skills.

To better protect the organization's computer-related assets from misuse, fraud, and unintentional actions, it is highly recommended that you PROHIBIT THE PERSONAL USE OF THE ORGANIZATION'S DATA, PROGRAMS, AND COMPUTER EQUIPMENT BY EMPLOYEES. If, however, you believe that the personal use of these assets of the organization is desirable and not precluded by other policies and regulations, develop and implement a program to control their use; this should include a realistic policy to define which resources may be used, who may use them, and for what purpose they may be used; and install appropriate accounting and auditing procedures to control the personal useage.

The computer security policy of the City of New York, figure 8-4, is provided as an example.

8.3.3 Make Appropriate Resources Available

Resources—people and funding—will be required to prevent computer-related losses. The level of resource commitment required for a cost-effective computer security program must be such that the cost of the security measures does not exceed the benefits derived from the security measures. The best way to define the appropriate resource level will be with the use of a quantitative risk analysis procedure. However, consider using qualitative risk analysis techniques to get you started sooner if your management is not yet ready to accept quantitative risk analysis costs or methodologies.

THE CITY OF NEW YORK
OFFICE OF THE MAYOR
NEW YORK, N.Y. 10007

DIRECTIVE TO ALL HE*DS OF AGENCIES AND DEPARTMENTS

No. 81-2

June 24 1981

Electronic Data Processing Security

Statement of Policy

The City of New York relies heavily on its
electronic data processing ("EDP") systems to meet its
operational, financial and informational requirements.
It is essential that these systems be protected from
misuse and that both the computer systems and the data
that they process be operated and maintained in a secure
environment. The Office of Operations and the Department
of Investigation are directed to work closely with agency
heads, heads of information services and Inspectors General to ensure that this is accomplished and that obser-
vations of computer fraud and misuse are reported in
accordance with the requirements of Executive Order No.
16(1978).

        1. All use of City owned or leased computer
systems must be for officially authorized purposes only.
Agency heads shall be responsible for the proper authorization of computer utilization by their agencies and
the establishment of effective use.

        2. The Commissioner of Investigation shall
establish City-wide standards for EDP security to ensure
that programs, data files and data communications as well
as City computer systems are used in compliance with this
Directive.

        3. The use of City computer systems for non-
City consulting work or other unofficial purposes is
prohibited without the written approval of the responsible agency head and the consent of the Corporation
Counsel.

Figure 8-4.

-2-

       4. The sale of City computer system time to persons or organizations other than City employees or agencies is prohibited without the prior written approval of the responsible agency head and the consent of the Corporation Counsel.

       5. All computer programs and data in City computer systems and data libraries are for the sole use of the City. All computer programs and data developed for the City by consultants to the City or provided to consultants for use in conjunction with programs or data developed for the City are the property of the City and must be promptly returned to the City upon project completion or termination, unless requested prior thereto by the agency head or the agency head's deisgnee.

       6. Copies of any programs or data may only be released from City computer systems upon written authorization of the agency head or the agency head's deisgnee.

       7. Effective immediately, all information services contracts, leases, licenses or other information services agreements entered into by the City shall contain a provision, approved as to form by the Corporation Counsel, advising information services vendors of the City's retained property rights with respect to its information systems, programs and data and the City's requirements for EDP security, including data maintenance and return.

       8. Passwords and other EDP security procedures shall be protected by individual users from unauthorized use or disclosure.

       9. Employees whose employment is terminated shall return all City property and equipment used in connection with City computer systems. Such items as keys, identification cards and badges, portable computer and communications equipment, manuals and documentation and other materials shall be returned to the individual employee's supervisor prior to the last day of active employment. It is recommended that agency heads refer to "System Security Standard No. 116," a copy of which is attached to this Directive, on this subject.

Figure 8-4, continued.

-3-

10. A violation of procedures established
pursuant to this Directive may result in the initiation
of disciplinary procedures. Misuse of government property, including programs and data, may also be punishable
by fine or imprisonment or both.

11. All City employees and vendors to the
City are hereby directed to remove immediately all unofficial data files and programs from City computer
systems. Questions concerning the appropriateness of
a data file or computer program shall be directed to
the individual employee's supervisor or to the responsible
agency head.

12. This Directive shall take effect immediately.

Edward I. Koch
M A Y O R

Figure 8-4, continued.

8.4 NBS APPLICATION SYSTEM VULNERABILITY CONSIDERATIONS

The National Bureau of Standards (FIPS Pub. 65, p. 22-27)[9] has compiled a list of application system vulnerabilities which are applicable to both federal government and private industry risk analysis. That list is provided in this section in its entirety.

APPENDIX

A. APPLICATION SYSTEM VULNERABILITIES

It will be useful to the team, as they consider applications systems and data files, to be aware of the many undesirable events which can have serious consequences. A number of situations to which applications systems are vulnerable are listed here, grouped according to common system organizational structures. The list is not intended to be all-inclusive but only to suggest the various kinds of vulnerabilities that may exist in each system.

1. ERRONEOUS OR FALSIFIED DATA INPUT. Erroneous or falsified input data is the simplest and most common cause of undesirable performance by an applications system. Vulnerabilities occur wherever data is collected, manually processed, or prepared for entry to the computer.

- Unreasonable or inconsistent source data values may not be detected.
- Keying errors during transcription may not be detected.
- Incomplete or poorly formatted data records may be accepted and treated as if they were complete records.
- Records in one format may be interpreted according to a different format.
- An employee may fraudulently add, delete, or modify data (e.g., payment vouchers, claims) to obtain benefits (e.g., checks, negotiable coupons) for himself.
- Lack of document counts and other controls over source data or input transactions may allow some of the data or transactions to be lost without detection—or allow extra records to be added.
- Records about the data-entry personnel (e.g., a record of a personnel action) may be modified during data entry.

- Data which arrives at the last minute (or under some other special or emergency condition) may not be verified prior to processing.
- Records in which errors have been detected may be corrected without verification of the full record.

2. MISUSE BY AUTHORIZED END USERS. End users are the people who are served by the ADP system. The system is designed for their use, but they can also misuse it for undesirable purposes. It is often very difficult to determine whether their use of the system is in accordance with the legitimate performance of their job.

- An employee may convert Government information to an unauthorized use; for example, he may sell privileged data about an individual to a prospective employer, credit agency, insurance company, or competitor; or he may use Government statistics for stock market transactions before their public release.
- A user whose job requires access to individual records in a file may manage to compile a complete listing of the file and then make unauthorized use of it (e.g., sell a listing of employees' home addresses as a mailing list).
- Unauthorized altering of information may be accomplished for an unauthorized end user (e.g., altering of personnel records).
- An authorized user may use the system for personal benefit (e.g., theft of services).
- A supervisor may manage to approve and enter a fraudulent transaction.
- A disgruntled or terminated employee may destroy or modify records—possibly in such a way that backup records are also corrupted and useless.
- An authorized user may accept a bribe to modify or obtain information.

---

[9]Guideline For Automatic Data Processing Risk Analysis, (FIPS PUB. 65), National Bureau of Standards, 8/1/79.

3. UNCONTROLLED SYSTEM ACCESS. Organizations expose themselves to unnecessary risk if they fail to establish controls over who can enter the ADP area, who can use the ADP system, and who can access the information contained in the system.

- Data or programs may be stolen from the computer room or other storage areas.
- ADP facilities may be destroyed or damaged by either intruders or employees.
- Individuals may not be adequately identified before they are allowed to enter ADP area.
- Remote terminals may not be adequately protected from use by unauthorized persons.
- An unauthorized user may gain access to the system via a dial-in line and an authorized user's password.
- Passwords may be inadvertently revealed to unauthorized individuals. A user may write his password in some convenient place, or the password may be obtained from card decks, discarded printouts, or by observing the user as he types it.
- A user may leave a logged-in terminal unattended, allowing an unauthorized person to use it.
- A terminated employee may retain access to ADP system because his name and password are not immediately deleted from authorization tables and control lists.
- An unauthorized individual may gain access to the system for his own purposes (e.g., theft of computer services or data or programs, modification of data, alteration of programs, sabotage, denial of services).
- Repeated attempts by the same user or terminal to gain unauthorized access to the system or to a file may go undetected.

4. INEFFECTIVE SECURITY PRACTICES FOR THE APPLICATION. Inadequate manual checks and controls to insure correct processing by the ADP system or negligence by those responsible for carrying out these checks result in many vulnerabilities.

- Poorly defined criteria for authorized access may result in employees not knowing what information they, or others, are permitted to access.
- The person responsible for security may fail to restrict user access to only those processes and data which are needed to accomplish assigned tasks.
- Large funds disbursements, unusual price changes, and unanticipated inventory usage

may not be reviewed for correctness.

- Repeated payments to the same party may go unnoticed because there is no review.
- Sensitive data may be carelessly handled by the application staff, by the mail service, or by other personnel within the organization.
- Post-processing reports analyzing system operations may not be reviewed to detect security violations.
- Inadvertent modification or destruction of files may occur when trainees are allowed to work on live data.
- Appropriate action may not be pursued when a security variance is reported to the system security officer or to the perpetrating individual's supervisor; in fact, procedures covering such occurrences may not exist.

5. PROCEDURAL ERRORS WITHIN THE ADP FACILITY. Both errors and intentional acts committed by the ADP operations staff may result in improper operational procedures, lapsed controls, and losses in storage media and output.

Procedures and Controls:

- Files may be destroyed during data base reorganization or during release of disk space.
- Operators may ignore operational procedures; for example, by allowing programmers to operate computer equipment.
- Job control language parameters may be erroneous.
- An installation manager may circumvent operational controls to obtain information.
- Careless or incorrect restarting after shutdown may cause the state of a transaction update to be unknown.
- An operator may enter erroneous information at CPU console (e.g., control switch in wrong position, terminal user allowed full system access, operator cancels wrong job from queue).
- Hardware maintenance may be performed while production data is on-line and the equipment undergoing maintenance is not isolated.
- An operator may perform unauthorized acts for personal gain (e.g., make extra copies of competitive bidding reports, print copies of unemployment checks, delete a record from journal file).
- Operations staff may sabotage the computer (e.g., drop pieces of metal into a terminal).

- The wrong version of a program may be executed.
- A program may be executed using wrong data or may be executed twice using the same transactions.
- An operator may bypass required safety controls (e.g., write rings for tape reels).
- Supervision of operations personnel may not be adequate during non-working hour shifts.
- Due to incorrectly learned procedures, an operator may alter or erase the master files.
- A console operator may override a label check without recording the action in the security log.

Storage Media Handling:
- Critical tape files may be mounted without being write protected.
- Inadvertently or intentionally mislabeled storage media are erased. In a case where they contain backup files, the erasure may not be noticed until it is needed.
- Internal labels on storage media may not be checked for correctness.
- Files with missing or mislabeled expiration dates may be erased.
- Incorrect processing of data or erroneous updating of files may occur when card decks have been dropped, partial input decks are used, write rings mistakenly are placed in tapes, paper tape is incorrectly mounted, or wrong tape is mounted.
- Scratch tapes used for jobs processing sensitive data may not be adequately erased after use.
- Temporary files written during a job step for use in subsequent steps may be erroneously released or modified through inadequate protection of the files or because of an abnormal termination.
- Storage media containing sensitive information may not get adequate protection because operations staff is not advised of the nature of the information content.
- Tape management procedures may not adequately account for the current status of all tapes.
- Magnetic storage media that have contained very sensitive information may not be degaussed before being released.
- Output may be sent to the wrong individual or terminal.
- Improperly operating output or post-processing units (e.g., bursters, decollators or multipart forms) may result in loss of output.
- Surplus output material (e.g., duplicates of

output data, used carbon paper) may not be disposed of properly.
- Tapes and programs that label output for distribution may be erroneous or not protected from tampering.

6. PROGRAM ERRORS. Applications programs should be developed in an environment that requires and supports complete, correct, and consistent program design, good programming practices, adequate testing, review, and documentation, and proper maintenance procedures. Although programs developed in such an environment will still contain undetected errors, programs not developed in this manner will probably be rife with errors. Additionally, programmers can deliberately modify programs to produce undesirable side effects or they can misuse the programs they are in charge of.

- Records may be deleted from sensitive files without a guarantee that the deleted records can be reconstructed.
- Programmers may insert special provisions in programs that manipulate data concerning themselves (e.g., payroll programmer may alter his own payroll records).
- Data may not be stored separately from code with the result that program modifications are more difficult and must be made more frequently.
- Program changes may not be tested adequately before being used in a production run.
- Changes to a program may result in new errors because of unanticipated interactions between program modules.
- Program acceptance tests may fail to detect errors that only occur for unusual combinations of input (e.g., a program that is supposed to reject all except a specified range of values actually accepts an additional value).
- Programs, the contents of which should be safeguarded, may not be identified and protected.
- Code, test data with its associated output, and documentation for certified programs may not be filed and retained for reference.
- Documentation for vital programs may not be safeguarded.
- Programmers may fail to keep a change log, to maintain back copies, or to formalize recordkeeping activities.
- An employee may steal programs he is maintaining and use them for personal gain (e.g., sale to a commercial organiza-

tion, hold another organization for extortion).

- Poor program design may result in a critical data value being initialized twice. An error may occur when the program is modified to change the data value—but only changes it in one place.
- Production data may be disclosed or destroyed when it is used during testing.
- Errors may result when the programmer misunderstands requests for changes to the program.
- Errors may be introduced by a programmer who makes changes directly to machine code.
- Programs may contain routines not compatible with their intended purpose, which can disable or bypass security protection mechanisms. For example, a programmer who anticipates being fired inserts code into a program which will cause vital system files to be deleted as soon as his name no longer appears in the payroll file.
- Inadequate documentation or labeling may result in wrong version of program being modified.

7. OPERATING SYSTEM FLAWS.
Design and implementation errors, system generation and maintenance problems, and deliberate penetrations resulting in modifications to the operating system can produce undesirable effects in the application system. Flaws in the operating system are often difficult to prevent and detect.

- User jobs may be permitted to read or write outside assigned storage area.
- Inconsistencies may be introduced into data because of simultaneous processing of the same file by two jobs.
- An operating system design or implementation error may allow a user to disable audit controls or to access all system information.
- The operating system may not protect a copy of information as thoroughly as it protects the original.
- Unauthorized modification to the operating system may allow a data entry clerk to enter programs and thus subvert the system.
- An operating system crash may expose valuable information such as password lists or authorization tables.
- Maintenance personnel may bypass security controls while performing maintenance work. At such times the system is vulnerable to errors or intentional acts of the maintenance personnel, or anyone else who

might also be on the system and discover the opening (e.g., microcoded sections of the operating system may be tampered with or sensitive information from on-line files may be disclosed).
- An operating system may fail to record that multiple copies of output have been made from spooled storage devices.
- An operating system may fail to maintain an unbroken audit trail.
- When restarting after a system crash, the operating system may fail to ascertain that all terminal locations which were previously occupied are still occupied by the same individuals.
- A user may be able to get into monitor or supervisory mode.
- The operating system may fail to erase all scratch space assigned to a job after the normal or abnormal termination of the job.
- Files may be allowed to be read or written without having been opened.

8. COMMUNICATIONS SYSTEM FAILURE.
Information being routed from one location to another over communication lines is vulnerable to accidental failures and to intentional interception and modification by unauthorized parties.

Accidental Failures:
- Undetected communications errors may result in incorrect or modified data.
- Information may be accidentally misdirected to the wrong terminal.
- Communication nodes may leave unprotected fragments of messages in memory during unanticipated interruptions in processing.
- Communication protocol may fail to positively identify the transmitter or receiver of a message.

Intentional Acts:
- Communications lines may be monitored by unauthorized individuals.
- Data or programs may be stolen via telephone circuits from a remote job entry terminal.
- Programs in the network switching computers may be modified to compromise security.
- Data may be deliberately changed by individuals tapping the line (requires some sophistication, but is applicable to financial data).
- An unauthorized user may "take over" a computer communication port as an au-

thorized user disconnects from it. Many systems cannot detect the change. This is particularly true in much of the currently available communication equipment and in many communication protocols.

- If encryption is used, keys may be stolen.
- A terminal user may be "spoofed" into providing sensitive data.
- False messages may be inserted into the system.
- True messages may be deleted from the system.
- Messages may be recorded and replayed into the system ("Deposit $100" messages).

chapter **9**

What to Do
When You Are
Victimized

This chapter deals with intentional computer abuse. It describes commonly used computer fraud techniques and provides a realistic method for dealing with both the abuse investigation and the apprehended abuser.

Don't assume from this chapter that intentional fraud by computer is rampant. Recognize that it is a reality that you must be prepared to combat with an aggressive security program that reduces vulnerabilities, and be ready to do battle with criminals.

9.1 HOW TO IDENTIFY A COMPUTER-RELATED LOSS OR ABUSE

Skillfully executed computer-related losses or abuses are difficult to detect or identify at the time of occurrence because they may be invisible. The loss becomes apparent at a later time. This may be the result of a recordkeeping difficulty, a problem reported by a customer of the organization, or from an informant. Some frauds may also be uncovered during routine audits, but this is not common.

Computer Crime: Criminal Justice Resource Manual (pp. 9-28) describes twelve computer-related crime methods in detail. These are excerpted below.[1]

1. Data Diddling

This is the simplest, safest, and most common method used in computer related crime. It involves changing data before or during their input to computers. The changing can be done by anybody associated with or having access to the processes of creating, recording, transporting, encoding, examining, checking, converting, and transforming data that ultimately enter a computer.

2. Trojan Horse

The Trojan horse method is the covert placement of computer instructions in a program so that the computer will perform unauthorized functions but usually still allow the program to perform its intended purposes. This is the most common method in computer program based frauds and sabotage. Instructions may be placed in production computer programs so that they will be executed in the protected or restricted domain of the program and have access to all of the data files that are assigned exclusive use of the program. Programs are usually constructed loosely enough to allow space to be found or created for inserting the instructions.

There are no practical methods of preventing and detecting Trojan horse methods if the perpetrator is sufficiently clever.

3. Salami Techniques

An automated form of crime involving the theft of small amounts of assets from a large number of sources is identified as a salami technique (taking small slices without noticeably reducing the whole). For example, in a banking system the demand deposit accounting system for checking accounts could be changed (using the Trojan horse method) to randomly reduce a few hundred accounts by ten cents or fifteen cents by transferring the money to a favored account where it can be legitimately withdrawn through normal methods. No

---

[1]Computer Crime: Criminal Justice Resource Manual, U.S. Department of Justice (027-000-00870-4), 1979.

Parts of Sections 9.1 and 9.3 have been excerpted from the Criminal Justice Resource Manual because it has become a much referenced standard and the recommended procedural steps represent sound investigative techniques. Expect to see investigative procedure changes as microcomputer-based investigative tools become available in the next few years.

The quoted sections, which are used by permission, are based on the work of Donn Parker of SRI International, and Susan Nycum of Gaston Snow and Ely Bartlett. They also appear in Mr. Parker's books *Computer Security Management*, Reston Publishing, 1981, and *Crime by Computer*, Charles Scribner's Sons, 1976.

controls are violated because the money is not removed from the system of accounts. Instead, a small fraction of it is merely rearranged. The success of the fraud is based on the idea that each checking account customer loses so little that it is of little consequence. Many variations are possible. The assets may be an inventory of products or services as well as money.

One salami method in a financial system is known as the "round down" fraud. The round down fraud requires a computer system application where large numbers of financial accounts are processed. The processing must involve the multiplication of dollar amounts by numbers—such as in interest rate calculations. This arithmetic results in products that contain fractions of the smallest denomination of currency, such as the cent. [These amounts are then applied to an account which is controlled by the perpetrators.].

4. Superzapping

Superzapping [also known as zapping] derives its name from superzap, a macro/utility program used in most IBM computer centers as a systems tool. Any computer center that has a secure computer operating mode needs a "break glass in case of emergency" computer program that will bypass all controls to modify or disclose any of the contents of the computer. Computers sometimes stop [processing], malfunction or enter a state that cannot be overcome by normal recovery or restart procedures. Computers also perform unexpectedly and need attention that normal access methods do not allow. In such cases, a universal access program is needed. This is similar in one way to a master key to be used if all other keys are lost or locked in the enclosure they were meant to open. [The superzap program permits the user to modify data or programs without leaving an audit trail.]

5. Trap Doors

In the development of large application and computer operating systems, it is the practice of programmers to insert debugging aids that provide breaks in the code for insertion of additional code and intermediate output capabilities. The design of computer operating systems attempts to prevent both access to them and insertion of code or modification of code. Consequently, system programmers will sometimes insert code that allows compromise of these requirements during the debugging phases of program development and later when the system is being maintained and improved. These facilities are referred to as trap doors. Normally, trap doors are eliminated in the final editing but sometimes they are overlooked or purposely left in to facilitate ease of making future access and modification. In addition, some unscrupulous programmers may purposely introduce trap doors for later compromising of computer programs. Designers of large complex programs may also introduce trap doors inadvertently through weaknesses in design logic.

Trap doors may also be introduced in the electronic circuitry of computers. For example, not all of the combinations of codes may be assigned to instructions found in the computer and documented in the programming manuals. When these unspecified commands are used, the circuitry may cause the execution of unanticipated combinations of functions that allow compromise of the computer system.

6. Logic Bombs

A logic bomb is a computer program executed at appropriate or periodic times in a computer system that determines conditions or states of the computer that facilitate the perpetration of an unauthorized, malicious act.

[A logic bomb can be programmed to trigger an act based on any specified condition or data that may occur or be introduced. Logic bombs may be placed in the computer system using the Trojan horse technique.]

7. Asynchronous Attacks

Asynchronous attack techniques take advantage of the asynchronous functioning of a computer operating system. Most computer operating systems function asynchronously based on the services that must be performed for the various computer programs in execution in the computer system. For example, several jobs may simultaneously call for output reports to be produced. The operating system stores these requests and, as resources become available, performs them in the order in which resources are available to fit the request or according to an overriding priority indication. Therefore, rather than executing requests in the order they are received, the system performs them asynchronously based on resources available.

8. Scavenging

Scavenging is a method of obtaining information that may be left in or around a computer system after the execution of a job. Simple physical scavenging could be the searching of trash barrels for copies of discarded computer listings or carbon paper from multiple-part forms. More technical and sophisticated methods of scavenging can be done by searching for residual data left in a computer after job execution.

For example, a computer operating system may not properly erase buffer storage areas used for the temporary storage of input or output data. Some operating systems do not erase magnetic disk or magnetic tape storage media because of the excessive computer time required to do this. Therefore, new data are written over the old data.

It may be possible for the next job to be executed to read the old data before they are replaced by new data.

9. <u>Data Leakage</u>

Several techniques can be used to leak data from a computer system. The perpetrator may be able to hide the sensitive data in otherwise innocuous looking output reports. This could be done by adding to blocks of data. In more sophisticated ways the data could be interspersed with otherwise innocuous data. An even more sophisticated method might be to encode data to look like something different than they are. For example, a computer listing may be formatted so that the secret data are in the form of different lengths of printer lines, number of words or numbers per line, locations of punctuation, and use of code words that can be interspersed and converted into meaningful data.

10. <u>Piggybacking and Impersonation</u>

Piggybacking and impersonation can be done physically or electronically. Physical piggybacking is a method for gaining access to controlled access areas when control is accomplished by electronically or mechanically locked doors. Typically an individual usually with his hands full of computer-related objects such as tape reels stands by the locked door. When an authorized individual arrives and opens the door, the piggybacker goes in after or along with him. Turnstyles, mantraps, or a stationed guard are the usual methods of preventing this type of unauthorized access. The turnstyle allows passage of only one individual with a metal key, an electronic or magnetic card key, or combination lock activation. A mantrap is a double-doored closet through which only one person can move with one key action. Success of this method of piggybacking is dependent upon the quality of the access control mechanism and the alertness of authorized persons in resisting cooperation with the perpetrator.

Electronic piggybacking can take place in an on-line computer system where individuals are using terminals, and identification is verified automatically by the computer system. When a terminal has been activated, the computer authorized access, usually on the basis of a key, secret password, or other passing of required information (protocol). Compromise of the computer can take place when a hidden computer terminal is connected to the same line through the telephone switching equipment and used when the legitimate user is not using his terminal. The computer will not be able to differentiate or recognize the two terminals, but senses only one terminal and one authorized user. Piggybacking can also be accomplished when the user signs off improperly, leaving the terminal in an active state or leaving the computer in a state where it assumes the user is still active. Impersonation is the process of one person assuming the identity of another. Physical access to computers or computer terminals and electronic access through terminals to a computer require positive identification of an authorized user.

11. Wire Tapping

There is no verified experience of data communications wire tapping. The potential for wire tapping grows rapidly, however, as more computers are connected to communication facilities and increasing amounts of electronically stored assets are transported from computer to computer over communication circuits. Wire tapping has not become popular as far as is known because of the many easier ways to obtain or modify data.

12. Simulation and Modeling

A computer can be used as a tool or instrument of a crime for planning or control. Complex white-collar crime often requires the use of a computer because of its sophisticated capabilities. An existing process can be simulated on a computer or a planned method for carrying out a crime could be modeled to determine its possible success.

The Criminal Justice Resource Manual's descriptions of computer-related crime methods deal primarily with criminal activities directed at the taking of assets that are controlled by computerized records. The assets obtained in this manner are principally money and data.

There are three other types of intentional computer-related abuses. They are theft of service, copying computer programs, and intentional data or computer program damage or destruction.

Theft of Service

Theft of service is the diversion of another person's computer processing services for the gain of the perpetrator. It may not be an illegal activity because many states do not have laws that specifically deal with computer services.

Theft-of-service incidents are probably the most common form of petty abuse involving computer systems. Employers normally handle theft-of-service abuses administratively or ignore them, based on my experiences and those of computer security colleagues. The most notable exception occurred in New York State where two individuals were thought to have diverted $200,000 worth of processing services. Those two individuals were successfully prosecuted.

Computer hackers, individuals who invade your computer system, may attempt to divert your processing resources, copy your data and/ or programs, damage or destroy your data, or simply embarrass you. Statistics are not available on hackers as they are a new type of criminal.

Copying Computer Programs

The unauthorized copying of computer programs, particularly by microcomputer users, has become a major source of revenue loss to program developers. Program developers are now beginning to litigate for substantial damages.

Program copying was not a significant problem during the late 1970s, when the Criminal Justice Resource Manual was prepared, because there were not enough microcomputers available to make it a significant crime. The largest settlement as of this writing was for several million dollars for infringing on another company's operating system software.

Intentional Data or Program Damage

Intentional data or program damage, like theft of service, may or may not be a criminal activity, depending on the jurisdiction and the method used to effect the abuse. The lack of state laws and the absence of federal statutes make prosecution difficult in this situation.

Intentional data and program damage is rarely reported, but poses a serious organizational threat. It may be effected by placing Trojan horse instructions in a program, using superzap techniques or simply by using utility programs to modify or delete data records or files.

9.2 WHEN TO CALL FOR HELP

Computer-related loss and abuse are not as easy to deal with as the loss of physical assets. It is not always possible to determine if a loss has occurred, the extent of the loss, or the vulnerability of the organization to additional losses.

As an example, I was once asked to conduct an investigation of a licensing revenue application system that processed about ten million dollars per year. The lengthy investigation determined only that a possible loss of several hundreds of dollars might have occurred. Even that loss was speculative; records necessary for the investigation were not available because of a severe breakdown of system controls and procedures.

The difficulties with the system included poor reconciliation procedures, poor license issuance controls, an almost undocumented computer application system, and a poor segregation of people functions. Faced with a situation like this, and a very small documented possible loss, it is more beneficial to remedy the problem than to expend considerable further resources on an investigation where the probability of a successful case closing is virtually nonexistent.

This is not an atypical situation for any organization that has a large number of older computer applications that are still in use because they work, but were stripped of controls to make sure that operational problems did not arise. A call for help under similar circumstances in your organization would probably yield similar results.

This example was not intended to discourage a potential victim from reporting a suspected loss to the organization's management. Rather, it was intended to demonstrate the need for immediate notification when a computer-related problem becomes apparent, and the need to maintain and enforce adequate controls.

Records related to a computer loss are critical to any investigation of the loss. They must be preserved and protected in advance of any problem so that they will be available if a problem arises.

To get back to the objective of this section, the time to call for help with a computer-related loss is before the loss occurs. Do that by critically examining your application systems and asking your staff and yourself which systems are most vulnerable to fraud and abuse.

From a logical point of view, systems that dispense money are the most obvious targets for criminal gain actions. Look at the oldest systems first. Try to detect those controls that are absent or that have been deactivated.

Sensitive data or computer programs that could be sold may be equally as important as money to your organization. Determine if they are adequately protected. Again, as with money systems, look for ways that data or programs could be stolen.

Do not omit revenge as a motivator that may be as strong or stronger than financial gain as incentive to abuse your system, data, and programs. Look for the places where someone could harm your organization in either a straightforward or a convuluted manner.

Call for help when you find a vulnerability that is obvious and easy to exploit. The help may be your staff and/or the EDP audit staff.

Call for help immediately if you find any indication of an actual loss or abuse. Your computer security officer should be contacted first. You may also need your security department, legal department, and the EDP audit department.

9.3 HOW TO COLLECT EVIDENCE

The successful prosecution of a computer-related fraud or abuse case will require that evidence be obtained to prove that a loss occurred and that the accused individual(s) is responsible. Simply stated, evidence is that which is submitted to ascertain the truth of the matter. The evidence must meet strict requirements to be admissible in a court of law. Evidential requirements may be less stringent where an organization does not wish to prosecute an employee but rather chooses to handle the matter as a disciplinary procedure.

As a manager, you may not know where an abuse investigation may lead. The most practical approach to the collection of initial evidence is to request guidance from your security and legal departments prior to consulting with law enforcement officials.

Once you request law enforcement assistance, you may lose control of the evidence-gathering process. You may also expect to have your computer operations briefly disrupted.

The Criminal Justice Resource Manual cited earlier (pp. 100-113) provides the following specific considerations and procedures for the collection and preservation of computer-related evidence.

COMPUTER EVIDENCE CONSIDERATIONS
As in the preparation of any case for prosecution, the use of evidence is a significant element.
The most likely of the principal defense strategies that will arise in a computer-related crime case will be an attack on the admissibility of the prosecutor's computer or computer-generated physical evidence.

He should be alerted that perhaps in no other type of crime is an attack on admissibility of evidence more likely to succeed. The purpose here is to alert prosecutors to those potential evidence issues based on general law principles that are most likely to be used in computer-related crime cases and to encourage that preventive measures be taken during all investigative and prosecutive stages.

1. Search and Seizure

The nature of computer-related crime investigation frequently will require a search of a computer center or a remote computer terminal location, either as the situs of the crime or of the fruits of the crime. Equally likely will be the necessity to seize computer or computer-generated physical evidence as essential evidence for successful prosecution.

Thus, an entire pandora's box of legal issues becomes available to the defense, and the alert prosecutor must remain ever mindful of this potential. The nemesis here is the exclusionary rule that could well obliterate the prosecutor's case. Most search and seizure issues, such as consent, informers, entry and searches incident to detention and arrest generally will arise and apply much as they would in noncomputer-related cases.

In computer-related crime cases, search warrants should generally be obtained and used. Special consideration should be given, however, to situations providing application of exigent circumstance exceptions to preserve evidence because of the high degree of ease with which both instruments and fruits of the crime can rapidly destroy or alter computer evidence. Application of the plain view doctrine should be cautiously relied on. There is a strong likelihood that a defense will attempt to show the lack of sophistication of most prosecutors and investigators in computer technology.

Furthermore, avoid reliance on the use of an expert informant at the search scene to point out what items should be seized. California prosecutors are directed to *People* vs. *Superior Court* (Williams) 77 C.A. 3d 69 at page 78 for a discussion of this issue. Another problem with informers is that generally they will be insiders and are legally "untested" or "unreliable" as informers. Thus, be prepared to show sufficient corroboration of their information before preparation of the warrant or the search.

A difficult problem in drafting computer-related search warrants will be the tightrope walk between "reasonable particularity" in describing the items to be seized. Avoid, as much as possible, the necessity of seizing items not described in the warrant. A data processing expert will be necessary in drafting the warrant to ensure that all system hardware and program components are included.

The timeliness of the execution of the warrant may be critical. The avoidance of legal staleness of the information or other time constraints imposed by law is one objective balanced against the need of the prosecutor to obtain evidence of an operational fraud—i.e., a fraud that occurs only during an actual computer operation. The problem becomes more difficult when the operational fraud arises out of irregular computer usage.

Many more search and seizure "traps" may await the computer-related crime prosecutor. Therefore, be open to using imagination and ingenuity as well as the training and experience obtained in all computer-related search and seizure situations.

2. Obtaining Evidence

When a search calls for obtaining documents, they can be visually identified and computer technology expertise is not usually needed. Documents such as system manuals, computer run books, interpreted punch cards (with printed contents across the top), program documentation, logs, data and program input forms, and computer printed forms are usually labeled as to their contents. Whether they are complete, original, copies and match search needs can be determined by careful and complete questioning. Lack of cooperation of hostile custodians of documents may be overcome by separate questioning of individuals.

Requesting program documentation may require knowledge of computer program concepts to know the types and extent of documentation required—e.g., source listing, object listing, flowcharts, test data, storage dumps, etc. It must also be realized that program documentation is frequently obsolete relative to currently used versions of the programs. The latter must be obtained in new computer printouts. Program documentation is usually found in a centralized library. However, in some programming organizations the most recent documentation is in the possession of individual programmers and must be obtained from them or their offices. If there is any question about what may be obtained or identified, an expert should accompany the search officer.

Taking possession of other computer media materials may be more technically complex. Magnetic tapes and disks are normally externally labeled as to their contents, but a log or program documentation may be necessary to obtain full titles or descriptions given only the reel number or coded label. The program documentation must be for the program that produces or uses the tape. A large tape file may reside on more than one reel of tape (called volumes). It may be necessary to have a trusted technologist check the contents of a tape or disk by using a compatible computer and computer program.

Searching for information inside a computer can be highly complex and requires experts.... Preparing a search warrant for this also is complex and requires expert advice. Any materials that must be seized may also be required for continued operation of the computer center. If the intent is not to inhibit continued operation, a copy of the material may have to be made. If the copying is to be done at the searched facilities, a trusted person should be assigned to the task. It may be easy to destroy information before it can be removed; however, if it is destroyed in a computer center, there frequently will be backup copies stored in a remote backup facility.

The California Evidence Code now states that computer-generated evidence is the same as traditional evidence. However, the reliability and integrity of the computer-generated evidence must be proved. Computer-generated evidence can be the result of the work of several different technologists, including the systems analyst who designed and specified the computer program that produced the evidence, the programmers who wrote and tested the programs, the computer operators who operated the computer to run the programs that produces the report, the data preparations staff who prepared the data in computer-readable form (tape or disk), the tape librarian with the responsibility for supplying the correct tapes or disks containing the source data, the electronic maintenance engineer who maintains correct function of the hardware, the job setup clerk and job output clerk who are responsible for manual handling of the input and output before and after the job is run, and the system maintenance responsible for the integrity of the computer operating system used in the execution of the computer program.

It is better to use a generally known, accepted, and widely used computer program package as evidence rather than to have a special-purpose program developed or have some other special-purpose program that may be in the victim's possession. Generalized EDP audit packages are available from several program vendors and CPA firms. These programs should be used whenever possible. Logs and journals that provide records of the execution of the program should be obtained and initialed by the individuals responsible for the actions that result in these records.

The security efforts in safeguarding can be an important aspect in the investigation and prosecution of a suspected computer-related crime. If a computer organization has a security specialist..., he can be of great assistance in providing information concerning deviations from normal activities that might be associated with a suspected crime. His records could provide significant amounts of evidence that might be used in a criminal trial, primarily because they may be an exception to heresay [sic] evidence rules in that the records will frequently be produced in the normal course of business. The computer security specialist can quickly and easily brief an investigator or prosecutor on the safeguards that may be associated with or violated in a computer-related crime.

A computer security officer may have some of the following information files of use to the investigator:

- Audit reports filed by data and subject that could reveal vulnerabilities and problems.
- Computer operations exception reports of checkpoint restarts, missing tapes and output, data communications traffic errors, password and access failures.
- Loss experience reports of accidental and intentional acts.
- Assets lists including all computer equipment and programs, data files, supplies and facilities.
- Floor plans of all facilities.
- Maintenance records of safeguards and controls.
- Personnel summary files and listings.

There may be a problem, however, in convincing a victim to give up important evidence in the form of magnetic tape reels of master files and various materials needed to continue the business. This problem might easily be solved by having the victim make and use copies of the material. The prosecutor must be sure that he obtains the original material and not the copy because he would otherwise have to establish the integrity of the copying. (Author's Note: Data on nonremovable disks must be copied.)

The EDP auditor within the victim organization or from the external CPA organization that audits the victim organization can be of great help in assuring the integrity of the methods used in obtaining evidence....their function is to ensure the integrity of all data processing for victim organizations. The professional societies that these various auditors belong to often have certification programs and codes of ethics that may be used to assist in validating the integrity of the technologists who may be used.

Much can be gained from the negative experiences and complications of obtaining and introducing computer-related evidence in trials. This can be an aid for advising the potential victims of computer-related crime of the kinds of controls and safeguards that they should install to result in acceptable evidence in cases of these kinds.

Examples of safeguards are the labeling of computer programs and data, journaling of computer system activity, audit trails built into systems that result in reports that can be categorized as ordinary business reports, and retention of potential evidence for a reasonable period of time.

3. Computer Reports as Evidence

Data contained in the storage devices of a computer or in computer-readable media such as magnetic tape, punch cards, punch tape, removable disks, or electronic plug-in storage devices are frequently needed as evidence in human-readable form. Accomplishing the printing or display of data does not normally result in erasing or destroying the data in the computer or computer-readable media unless that is the intended purpose. However, if desired in this process, the storage device or media can be erased, the contained data replaced with other data, or physically destroyed, or made unusable. Normally, only copies of the desired data are obtained. The report production process is described in figure 1. [figure 9-1.] Occupations of people who participate in real-time and nonreal-time modes in the production of a report are also indicated.... This is important for the prosecutor who may need the testimony of such people to validate the integrity and correctness of the report-producing process.

a. Production Steps in an On-Line System Mode

In an on-line system, it is possible to obtain the report in two ways. The report may be produced at a terminal, or it may be requested from a terminal but printed at the computer site and delivered to the requester.... The steps in either case are as follows:

(1) Log on to an activated terminal with authorization and identity codes.

(2) Enter the system mode providing user interaction with the data file of interest.

(3) Request a copy of the data file or part of it by specifying its name, using formatting instructions and commands. This will cause the proper file to be accessed if it is on-line. If it is not available, a message will appear on the computer console printer or CRT informing the computer operator of a request for an off-line file. The computer operator will take action to make the file available in on-line mode. This may require assistance of a media librarian and a peripheral equipment operator. In the case of a magnetic tape file, the tape must be retrieved from the tape library adjacent to or near the computer peripheral equipment and mounted on a tape drive. The tape drive must be assigned with an address (usually a single digit). The address is either specified by the computer or must be typed into the console typewriter for the system to locate the source of the file.

(4) The file or selected part of it will be displayed on the CRT, printed on a printer at the terminal or printed at the computer site,

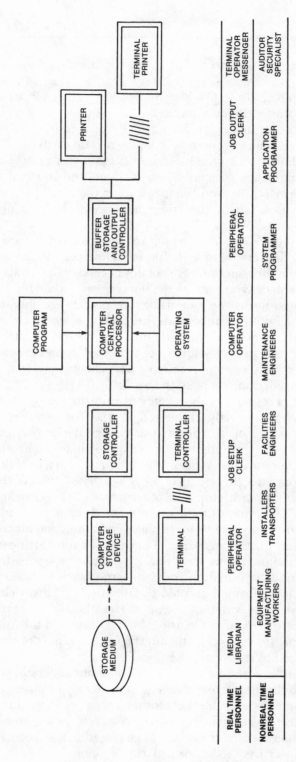

Figure 9-1. Production Process for Computer Reports

165

and delivered to the user according to the commands entered at the terminal.

b. Production Steps in an Off-Line System Mode (Batch Processing)

In a system where the data retrieval is to be performed in batch mode, the steps outlined below are normally performed.

(1) The user fills out a form to be key-punched on cards or directly prepares punch cards with the user identification and authorization information, file name, formatting instructions, and retrieval commands. The forms, cards, and file media (if in the user's possession) are submitted as a job at the computer service desk or proper receptacle.

(2) The job setup clerk puts the job request cards in a stack with other jobs and delivers them with file media or file media request forms to the computer operator. He obtains necessary file media such as tapes or disk packs from the media librarian as authorized by the file media request forms and mounts or directs a storage operator to mount the media on a peripheral device. The operator then enters commands at the console of the computer that causes the "stack" of jobs, including the subject job, to be processed consecutively but sharing the various system resources asynchronously (not consecutively) as needed to complete the work.

(3) The report containing the requested information comes from the output printer directly connected to the computer or it is produced and stored on a tape or disk storage device for off-line printing. The on-line printing may be performed in a spooling mode where the output is saved on tape or disk and printed at a later time in parallel with computer processing of other jobs. The output of the job usually is combined with output of other jobs run at approximately the same time. The printer produces the printed reports on continuous forms separated by one or more pages containing job identification, showing termination of output of one job and the starting of the next. The information consisting of a job number assigned by the computer at input is usually printed in large block letters 3 or 4 inches high that are formed graphically from printing many characters in patterns. This is done for ease of identification, separation, and stacking of the reports. Occasional errors occur in this process where the report for one job is still attached to the report of another job and delivered to the wrong user.

(4) The output report is placed with the job input materials, and all are returned to the user in one of several ways. It may be placed on an open shelf or in an open cubby hole for the user to pick up. It may be delivered to the user's office or an intermediate pickup site by a messenger. Sometimes the material will be placed in a locked cabinet for which the user has the key or lock combination.

c. Backup

Most computer centers have an automatic backup and recovery capability for all jobs, or it is provided at the request of the user.... If a report or computer-stored data used by a job are inadvertently destroyed, modified, or lost, they can be restored. This is done by saving the tape or disk on which the data were placed for a specified period of time, or on-line computer storage is periodically copied on to an archive backup tape or disk or on request of the user. The tape or disk is stored for a specified period of time in a media library and may be cycled through a remote backup facility, such as a bank vault or warehouse. Commercial services are sometimes used for this backup. The copying is done after each job or possibly each night or on weekends. When the option of backup is given to users, it is frequently not used because of cost or lack of other motivation. Another backup method is to microfilm and archive reports following similar procedures as with tape and disk.

d. Report-Producing Computer Programs

Generalized audit programs are frequently used to produce special reports.... Also report generator utility programs are normally available from within the operating system.... The data selected by naming the files, records and fields may be sorted into various sequences, reordered, and labeled in the required report formats. Data may be coded, formatted, and printed in any form desired; however, if available programs do not meet a specific need, a special program must be developed. Programmers often dislike this type of work and will resist requests for specialized output reports or say that it cannot be done. Reports can be obtained from any computer-readable data, in any format desired, in any desired order within the printer line length, line spacing, and character fonts available according to the printer used. It is only a question of size of effort, programmer skills, and cost.

e. Secure Report Production

Although the following instruction may seem far more elaborate than is practical, anything short of these methods in obtaining and using computer reports as evidence would be attacked by any opposing attorney. The only alternative is to obtain testimony of trustworthy experts to support the less elaborate methods that may be used.

Errors and omissions or malicious intentional acts are possible at each stage in the report-producing process or by nonreal-time program or data modification. Prevention or detection of sufficiently sophisticated intentional acts is often not possible on a practical basis. Therefore, varying degrees of precautions must be taken, and prosecutors must invoke the trust of data processing personnel, depending on potential threats and degree of confidence needed in the integrity and correctness of the report contents.

A moderate level of confidence can be obtained by taking the storage medium (tape or disk) to a different computer center to have its contents printed. Independence should be further ensured by verifying that personnel in the center would have no special interest in the work they would be required to do. Otherwise, the primary concern is to determine that a valid data source has been obtained.

The following steps also require a trusted computer user and/or one or more observers technically competent in all technical subjects that are identified. A handwritten log should be prepared describing each action taken, naming personnel involved, recording times and places, identifying materials, names, serial numbers of all equipment, computer programs used, and all results.

(1) Preparing the job for submission to the computer system requires obtaining the correct data source medium (tape, disk, cards, or storage device), a test data source in the same type of medium with a human-readable copy of the data, a trusted computer program, a trusted computer operating system, and a trusted computer system. Potential threats include substitution of the data or test sources, Trojan horse modification of the program or operating system, or electronic or mechanical modification of the computer system....A trusted manager of computer operations should be required to directly perform all actions or personally direct his staff. The data storage medium, if of a removable type (tape, disk, cards), should be positively identified as follows:

• Tape: Serial number usually in large block characters affixed by the computer center in which it was first used; tape reel label affixed to the side or flange of the reel identifying the current contents of the tape and usually a date on which the tape was last certified or tested; and an internal label with equivalent content identification and reel number recorded as the tape header or first record on the tape. The latter requires a computer program executed on a computer to determine the content of the label or header.
• Disk: External labels are similar to those for tapes. Internal labels are normally recorded at the beginning of each file of data on the disk or each band or sector.
• Punch cards: Handwritten descriptions of the contents are usually on the top of the deck, on the first card, or on the box containing the cards. The first card or first few cards may have the contents identification punched in them and can be visually read from the printing across the tops of the cards or by decoding the punches in them. Usually one or more cards at the back of the deck will identify

the end of the data. Normally, the last few columns of each data card will contain a sequence number and possibly content information in abbreviated form.

• On-Line storage: There is no way to visually identify the data directly. It can only be identified by execution of a computer program that caused the identification to be printed or displayed.

A trusted individual who knows as much as possible about the source of the data should verify the identity of the data and initial the storage medium on the external label. He should also observe the safekeeping of the medium and its usage before, during, and after its use. He should be aware that tape can be spliced, magnetically modified, and wound onto a different reel. A disk could be placed in a different cover or magnetically modified. Punch cards can be replaced, new holes punched, or existing holes covered over. There is no practical way to determine the integrity of data in on-line storage. The only assurance is based on the trustworthiness of all persons with the skills, knowledge, and access to modify the on-line data. This also is the case with removable media, once placed on a computer system storage device.

When the computer program is in a removable medium to be used in the same ways as the data identification described above, a trusted individual should identify it. The copy of the program should be obtained from an independent source where it would be free from tampering by any parties to the crime under investigation. The copy of the operating system and related utility programs should be obtained in the same way. A program and operating system already in on-line computer storage should not be used.

The job set-up process should be observed by the appropriate technical expert. All documents and new data storage media for job input purposes should be logged and initialed by the person supplying and using them.

Action can be taken to partially compensate for this greatest vulnerability of protecting integrity in the production of a report. If the original and computer design engineers programmers, maintenance programmers, and engineers are available, they can be consulted and their trustworthiness evaluated. This may be more practical for the report production program than for the operating system and computer system because these two systems can be so large that hundreds or even thousands of programmers and engineers are involved. It may also be possible to document the care taken in the design and implementation of the products used. Experts and state-of-the-art literature can be used to evaluate and establish reasonable care. Other users of the same products can also aid in determining the trustworthiness of products to be used. Finally, testing of the products can be done as described in the next step described below.

(2) In the computer usage steps, the first task is to reduce the computer system equipment that is on-line and the computer programs in the computer to the practical minimum necessary to produce the report. This may be costly in a large computer system because it requires paying for the entire system rather than sharing it with other users. Choosing a night or weekend period could help reduce cost or reduce the number of users sharing the system. Next, as much residual data and programs as possible should be erased from the system. This is usually too costly for large, secondary storage devices. The operating system should be refreshed in storage from the backup storage medium. The report producing job can then be run using the test data for which the human-readable version is available. The resulting output report can then be checked to assist in ensuring the integrity of the process. The job can then be run with the subject data to produce the desired report. The job could be run a second time to increase confidence by comparing the results.

(3) Independent, trustworthy observers with the skills and knowledge to determine correct operations should observe all production steps. Each person involved in producing the report should be identified and should initial the documentation of the materials used and records produced. Copies of all handwritten logs, journals, and computer-produced documents including the computer console printer log, should be collected.

(4) The information in the computer-produced report should be evaluated for reasonableness. All materials should be carefully preserved. This includes keeping data storage media in proper environments (within heat and humidity constraints). This is required for punch cards as well as magnetic media.

4. Caring for Evidence

Some types of computer-related evidence require special care. Storage environments must be controlled, and physical damage from manual handling must be avoided. Criminal justice agencies normally have evidence storage and archiving facilities, but these environments may not be suited to computer-related evidence and correct handling experience may be lacking. Types of evidence and special needs are described below:

• Magnetic tape and magnetic disk

Storage: 40 degrees F-90 degrees F, 20%-80% RH (80 degrees F Wet Bulb Max.). Unrecorded tape or disk may be stored up to 120 degrees F (90 degrees F Wet Bulb Max.). Storage life for data retention and recovery is 3 years.

Handling: Store, handle, and transport items in hard cover containers. Avoid dropping or squeezing. Always grasp by the hub; touch, bend, or crease no parts of the recording surfaces (the first 5 ft. or leader of tape can be handled and creased). Avoid placing near strong magnetic fields that might be created by a motor or permanent magnet. Affix tags or marks on containers or reel surfaces that do not come in contact with tape or disk drive equipment. Store tape reels vertically in tape storage racks and disk packs on flat wide shelves.

• Punch cards and punch paper tape

Storage: Same as magnetic tape. Storage life indefinite.

Handling: Avoid folding, spinning, or knicking edges. Never use paper clips or rubber bands. Store in metal or cardboard boxes in which they come from manufacturer. Store under mild pressure (in full boxes) to avoid warping. Jog card decks to align them in a job table (on top of card equipment). Wind tape on the tape winders only (some tape is accordion folded). Individual cards and pieces of tape can be handled manually, with care not to damage edges or tear. Tagging or marking methods are not critical. Avoid tape that removes paper surfaces or covers punched holes.

• Computer listings

Storage: No restrictions except to avoid strong light to reduce fading. Store on flat surfaces between covers (binders).

Handling: Continuous forms should be bursted into separate pages for ease in reading but not bursted if the continuous form nature of the listing is important to the case. Assure positive page sequence or numbering before bursting to assure correct page sequences. Some printers use special paper that may require special handling for preservation. There are no tagging or marking restrictions.

• Electronic and mechanical components

Storage and handling: Consult the manufacturer or owner for special instructions.

The owners of computer-related evidence may have special problems when the evidence is removed from their possession or custodianship as stated previously. The material may be necessary to continue their legitimate business or other activities. In such cases, the material should be copied in an appropriate, independent, and secure fashion and the *copy* returned to the rightful owner or user.

5. Privacy and Secrecy of Evidence

Evidence seized in the form of computer media may have data stored that are immaterial to the investigation but that may be confidential to the rightful owner. This could involve the issues of personal privacy, trade secrets, or government secrets. The problem may be solvable by retrieving and copying on another computer medium only the data at issue in the case. However, this frequently is not possible.

In such a case, it may be possible to give assurance that the extraneous data will not be revealed and will be stored in a secure manner that is at least as safe as where it was originally found.

Search and seizure right to privacy issues that arise generally can be handled by using the same principles in much the same way as in noncomputer abuse cases. As discussed earlier, the prosecutor should remain alert to these issues; again, taking preventive measures during search and seizure efforts is the best cure.

Nonsearch and seizure right to privacy issues will arise where personal, privileged, or classified information or transactions are involved and reflected on the proffered evidence. Obtaining consent from the individual(s) who are the subjects of the information is sometimes available.

Even where consent is not obtained, sufficient safeguards that are available in most jurisdictions minimize this problem. A hearing outside the presence of the jury or even an "in camera" hearing may allow the court to overrule the objection or perhaps excise the specific objectionable portions. With the exercise of such safeguards, the compelling state interest in law enforcement will generally prevail.

9.4 HOW TO STOP FURTHER LOSSES

Every computer-related abuse will cost your organization money. It will probably cause you some amount of visceral turmoil. It may result in unfavorable publicity for the organization, which is one reason that some companies choose not to prosecute computer abusers.

Once it becomes apparent that your organization has sustained a loss, it would be prudent for you to begin a confidential analysis of the loss and the conditions that made it possible for the loss to occur. The objectives of the analysis will be to define the extent of the loss, limit the impact of the loss, and to prevent the occurrence of future similar losses.

Specific areas to look at will include:

1. Controls Failure(s)

Adequate controls can not prevent all losses from occurring, but at a minimum they should provide a means to detect that a loss did occur and provide an audit trail to fix responsibility for the loss. Review the adequacy of the controls with respect to the incident and determine if additional controls are necessary on an interim basis during the investigation as well as after the investigation.

2. System Penetration

Determine the extent of system penetration by the perpetrator(s). Complex technical frauds may have involved changes to application and system software. A full review of all computer programs that the perpetrator worked on, or could have had access to, must be reviewed by qualified technicians. This may be a very time consuming activity.

Data files must be examined. This will be necessary for technical frauds as well as frauds that were accomplished by manipulating manual records that were used as input to computer systems. Account adjustments may be necessary.

3. Resources Required

The investigation process will require staff resources. These should be documented to help substantiate the extent of the loss. Typically, expect to include management personnel, security officers, data processing technicians, and EDP auditors.

You may also want to develop a projection of resources that will be required to undo any data or program changes that occurred.

4. Total Impact of the Loss

The total impact of the loss should be quantified. Law enforcement officials may only be interested in loss amounts that relate to the prosecution of the case. You and your management need the full loss costs, which include your investigative and error-correction costs, to evaluate the costs and benefits of adding additional controls.

9.5 DEALING WITH THE ABUSER

You will have to deal with the abuser during the investigation, and when it is over. This should not be a decision for the data processing manager. It is a business and personnel decision, not a data processing management decision.

1. During the Investigation

The most probable perpetrator of the fraud or abuse against the organization will be an employee. Employees have the knowledge of how the systems work, what controls exist, how to bypass the controls, and they have physical access to the system. Computer hackers are the obvious exceptions.

During an investigation, you may expect to be asked, or be required, to keep the suspect working at her present assignment, or you may not even initially know who the suspect is. This means that the organization will continue to be vulnerable to losses. The obvious business response would be to discharge the individual(s) and remedy the problem.

The investigator may need to apprehend the suspect in the act of committing the abuse, or need to document a series of incidents to determine the extent of the abuse. An appropriate organization official, not the investigator or the data processing manager, must decide if the continued level of risk is acceptable.

Once it becomes sufficiently apparent that a specific employee(s) is responsible for the fraud or abuse, the employee should be immediately suspended or discharged. This may occur in advance of an arrest, if a criminal statute has been violated.

The employment decision must be made on the basis of evidence necessary for the personnel action. Law enforcement officials may not want to release any case evidence that they have seized. Request permission to make and retain your own evidence copies. There are legal and personnel issues involved that go beyond the experience of most managers, and appropriate organization officials must participate in any employee termination procedure.

2. After the Investigation

Once the required evidence has been collected and the investigation has been concluded, you may find that in criminal cases the prosecutor may not want the suspect arrested immediately. This may occur because the legal system clock begins at the time of arrest and the case may require extensive analysis and preparation before an arrest is made. You may therefore be faced with a decision regarding an employee whom everyone thinks is guilty, but whom no one is ready to deal with.

Again, as with the during-the-investigation stage, the appropriate organization officials must be ready to take an action in accordance with the organization's policies and any applicable labor agreements. The most practical solution to this problem may be a suspension, with or without pay, for the suspect employee(s).

The key to dealing with the suspected employee(s) is to understand the extent and impact of the abuse and the suspect's involvement and plan accordingly. You may need the suspect's help and cooperation, yet you may not be comfortable in trusting the suspect if help is offered in return for dropped or reduced charges. You or the organization may or may not wish to dismiss the employee(s).

DON'T WAIT UNTIL THE INVESTIGATION HAS BEEN CON-CLUDED BEFORE YOU MAKE PLANS FOR DEALING WITH THE SUSPECTED ABUSER.

chapter **10**

How to Deal with Disruptions and Disasters

This chapter will help the business manager understand what EDP disruptions and disasters are and will provide suggestions for selling top management on the need for an effective disaster recovery plan. It includes key areas to be addressed by the plan and sample forms to help the disaster recovery planner get started developing the plan in a manner that will get top management support and approval.

An EDP disaster recovery plan is an organization's blueprint for containing service disruptions that could become disasters, and for recovering from those situations that could become disastrous to the organization. It must be more than a fat book in the data processing manager's library. The plan must be the daily procedures that are used to respond to emergency situations, and the tested procedures that would be used if the data center were to be destroyed or to become unavailable for processing the organization's vital information.

Building the specific disaster recovery plan for a data center in a large organization will require the dedicated services of one full-time planner for six to eighteen months, and the short-term assignment of specialists from many areas within the organization. Building a plan for multiple data centers will require considerably more time and resources.

The duration (calendar months) necessary to develop the initial plan can be shortened by using a consultant to write the plan. This can be a very effective quick start-up approach if the consultant develops the plan in conjunction with the staff disaster planner who will ultimately be responsible for ongoing plan testing and maintenance.

10.1 UNDERSTANDING DISRUPTIONS AND DISASTERS

Disruptions and disasters may be defined in terms of processing unavailability, damage to equipment and/or facilities, or consequences to the organization. Let's consider some general concepts that will enable you to develop definitions that are specific to your organization.

The National Bureau of Standards[1] suggests three categories—limited loss of capability, interruption to operations with little or no damage to the facility, and major damage or destruction of the facility and contents. These are summarized as:

"1. LIMITED LOSS OF CAPABILITY implies that only some systems will be affected."[2] Those systems will differ in time urgency and loss potential. For example, assume that a data center had two central processing units (CPUs), one for production system processing and a smaller one for application system development. The production CPU fails and the critical workload can be substantially processed by the development CPU. Normal operations would be interrupted, but critical system processing would not be initially disrupted if it were transferred to the application system development CPU.
Typical causes of limited loss of capabilities may also include:
a. Failure of key hardware units such as disk controllers, printers, and the like
b. Partial loss of air conditioning
c. Partial loss of communications equipment or circuits
d. Temporary loss or failure of data or key programs
"2. INTERRUPTION TO OPERATIONS with little or no facility damage, for a period sufficiently short to not significantly impact the organization."[3] An interruption, such as the total failure of electrical power or air conditioning systems, stops processing activities.

---

[1] *Guidelines for Automatic Data Processing Physical Security and Risk Management,* National Bureau of Standards, FIPS Publication 31, June, 1974, p. 67.

[2] Ibid.

[3] Ibid.

However, once power or air conditioning is restored, if no significant damage has occurred, operations can resume with priority restoration of critical application systems.

Typical causes of interruptions may include:

a. Labor disputes, demonstrations, civil commotion
b. Evacuation caused by bomb threat, gas leak, and the like
c. Short-term failure of key computer or communications equipment
d. Minor fire or flooding
e. Intrusion of smoke, dirt, dust

3. MAJOR DAMAGE to the facility or equipment may be a disaster for the data center but not the organization. The criticality of the applications to be processed and the ability to recover critical operations elsewhere are the key factors for reducing losses to the organization. Typical major damage causes may include:

a. Major fire in the computer room
b. Earthquake, general flood, tornado, building collapse
c. Bombing, explosion, aircraft crash
d. Contamination of the facility by radioactive or toxic materials.

The three categories described above can be reduced to terms of hours or days of processing unavailability that define a disruption and a disaster. Thus, a disaster may be defined as (1) The total destruction of a data processing facility; or (2) The total inability to process information for a period of three or more days; and a disruption becomes anything other than a disaster.

An alternative approach to defining disruptions and disasters is on the basis of the extent of a disruption to critical application system processing. A CRITICAL APPLICATION is one that must remain operational for the organization to survive, such as an on-line reservation system for a major airline. The definition of a disaster becomes the inability to process the critical application system(s) for a specified period of time, rather than the inability to process noncritical applications.

The critical application approach to defining disruptions and disasters makes the most sense from a management perspective. It can be used to express the real consequences to the organization when processing capabilities are interrupted. A methodology for identifying and quantifying critical applications is presented later in this chapter, together with sample forms for collecting information necessary to recover those applications.

10.2 SELLING DISASTER RECOVERY TO TOP MANAGEMENT

Disaster recovery planning must be mandated by top management or it will not succeed. Getting the mandate to develop an effective disaster recovery plan should be an easy task in the banking industry. The Comptroller of the Currency made disaster contingency planning review a board of directors' responsibility.[4]

> The Board of Directors of your bank must annually review and approve management's assessment of how a loss of EDP support would impact your bank's operations and the methods management has employed to reduce or eliminate such risk and/or impact. This annual review and approval must be noted in the minutes of the Board of Directors and will be verified at each examination of your institution.

Getting the mandate to develop an effective disaster recovery plan in other industries may require educating and selling management on the need to commit funding and personnel for something that may not happen. Use the resources within your organization and those that may be provided by external organizations to help you to get that "go-to-it" approval.

John Ratliff, Vice President of Marketing at Sungard Services Company, a well-known organization that provides disaster recovery processing and consulting services, suggested the following in his presentation "How to Sell Disaster Recovery to Top Management." It is reproduced with Mr. Ratliff's permission (pp. 1-6).

HOW TO SELL DISASTER RECOVERY TO TOP MANAGEMENT

by John Ratliff, Vice President of Marketing,
Sungard Services Company

In any discussion of how to sell a data processing disaster recovery program, it's important to know what you're selling. And to whom you're selling it. A comprehensive disaster recovery capability is, first and foremost, an insurance policy. It's a vital step in assuring the continuity of the single most important function a company has: the ability to run the business in a profitable manner utilizing data processing function. Without the

---

[4]Comptroller of the Currency, Administrator of National Banks, BC-177 (Revised), June 29, 1983, p. 2.

free exchange of information via computers through all departments of an organization, the company simply cannot operate in an
efficient, profitable way. Keep in mind that the data processing
function is the one system that permeates virtually all boundaries
within the corporate structure.

Don't make the mistake of thinking of disaster recovery as
strictly a data processing issue. It's much more than that. It is a
business issue; can the organization manage its business functions
in a profitable fashion over periods of time if it were suddenly faced
with the cessation of the DP operation? A comprehensive disaster
recovery program in reality safeguards a company's business
assets by maintaining its ability to make decisions; cash management decisions, inventory decisions, production decisions to name a
few. If a company's "nervous system" goes down, it's lost the
capacity to communicate both within and outside the corporate
walls.

Obviously, a disaster recovery plan must, in the end, be sold to
an organization's top management. Nothing will happen without
its buy-in. But there's a problem here—most levels of executive
management think that proper steps have been taken to assure DP
security. Conventional wisdom says that since it's a data processing
concern, the MIS department has taken care of it.

In many cases, it just isn't so. Usually it isn't the job of the MIS
manager to make the decisions—and spend the money—to install a
comprehensive security program. What most MIS managers do is
take steps that will assure continuity of operations from a production standpoint. To do this, he saves copies of operating systems and
backs up data files so that production can be resumed if a problem
occurs. But in just about every instance what the MIS department is
not prepared for is a devastation—the loss of the entire data center.

So, then, how should a disaster recovery plan be sold to top
management? A few years ago, fear was a popular approach. The
Foreign Corrupt Practices Act of 1977 helped things along by
mandating that a corporation take all prudent measures to protect
the corporate assets and to assure that the information be readily
available to stockholders, auditors and anyone else who had a legal
right to it. The act even named the corporation's chief financial
officer as the one executive who could be found criminally or civilly
negligent for failure to take corrective action to safeguard the
company's assets. The CFO, then, became the target of many selling
efforts.

Another variation of the fear tactic was trying to sell disaster
recovery on the basis of probability. But in many instances, this
approach doesn't cut much ice with top-level executives. Chances

are pretty good that they've been involved in the corporate structure for more than a few years and nothing catastrophic has happened yet to shut down the DP function. Besides, a CEO can make a strong case for rejecting the probability gambit by reminding the internal "salesman" of the great sums of money that have already been spent to build the data center fortress. "We installed the fire suppression you said you needed, we located out of the flood plain and out of hurricane alley, and now you say we have to spend more because something still may happen to it." No, selling top management on the probability of a disaster is doomed to failure.

Sell Prudence, Not Probability

The implementation of a comprehensive disaster recovery plan simply makes good business sense. There aren't many companies that do without a variety of other insurance programs, such as business interruption, and a complete recovery program should be viewed in the same light—as a cost of doing business.

As with other corporate insurance policies, disaster recovery should be analyzed from a consequences standpoint. Companies buy insurance on plants and machinery not because they think they're going to need it, but because they can't afford the consequences if they do lose it. If insurance were bought on a probability basis, the nation's insurance carriers would be looking for another line of work.

In fact, it's often a good idea to have top management compare the cost of a disaster recovery program against the level of consequences it is designed to guard against: the relative impact of the loss of the company's DP function and its ability to perform certain business functions for varying periods of time. When management makes this comparison of the recovery program premium against its coverage, it will probably find that it's the least expensive insurance policy it carries. Our experience has been that its cost is in the neighborhood of one percent of what other insurance plans cost.

Let's take a closer look at this statement. If, for example, a company is carrying $75 million in business interruption insurance, with a $1 million deductible, it isn't unusual for the premiums to be three to four million dollars a year. Compare that with a disaster recovery program where the losses could be much more devastating, say $200 million over a period of time. This plan's annual premiums typically run in the neighborhood of $150,000. So its cost is extremely modest compared to the coverage.

In some industries, banking for example, the loss of the data processing function for as few as three days could put them out of business. A large portion of a bank's assets are electronic. If it lost the ability to electronically manipulate money, e.g., transfer funds, it ceases to be a viable business. Quickly.

While a bank's inability to survive its DP loss for much more than three or four days may seem extreme, there are many manufacturing and service organizations that wouldn't stay afloat much longer. Remember, the losses caused by the absence of the DP function aren't of the straight-line variety; they have the habit of compounding themselves. A company's losses accumulate rapidly as it goes deeper into disaster mode because it's lost the ability to make good decisions to run its business profitability. It can lose market share, assets, and the capability of billing or collecting from customers. In fact, most manufacturing companies could better afford to lose one of its plants than its data processing function.

<u>Involve the Users</u>

The process of selling disaster recovery should involve the users—the real owners—of the data. The data processing department does not own the information it stores in its computer room; it is simply the data's custodian. The MIS manager, for example, is not accountable for the integrity of general ledger information. He <u>is</u> responsible for safeguarding it. If a disk crashes, it's his job to assure that all the corporate general ledger data is not destroyed. But the integrity of that information is an accounting function, or that of the various financial groups within the company. These are the people who should be addressed in the selling of disaster recovery because they are the ones who are most concerned about the loss of this information and the inability to process any of it.

Many organizations put their DP user groups through mock disasters: "OK, your DP function is gone, how do you intend to run your department?" Some companies even take their user groups offsite and force them to make operating decisions on the spot. And their ability to make effective decisions is tested.

If disaster recovery is most effectively sold to top management as an insurance plan that no prudent businessman should overlook, who should do the selling? Depending on the organization, it could be any one of a variety of people. An internal auditor is a typical salesman. Through the ongoing educational process, he's becoming more aware of the requirements and the need for protecting the company's assets. External auditing firms are another source. When they conduct a company audit they actively look for the existence of a disaster recovery plan. If one isn't in place they'll recognize this fact in their audit.

Obviously, the MIS manager can be a key proponent of a comprehensive recovery program. Depending to whom he reports, the MIS manager can direct his efforts to the company's CFO, its head of human resources, its VP of manufacturing, or even the CEO. And speaking of CEOs, it's not unusual for the more enlightened ones to initiate the question cycle downward through the organization: "What would we do if we lost our DP function?" If an inquisitive top executive doesn't like the answers that come back to him, he will often mandate a recovery plan. And since this one comes from the top down, chances are excellent that it will be a good one. Vendors of disaster recovery programs, despite their vested interests, can also be effective in selling the wisdom of this important form of business insurance.

The selling of disaster recovery is by no means an easy task. Despite the growing recognition of its importance, it's still another corporate expense that brings nothing to the bottom line. Whoever sells it, interested parties inside or outside of the organization, should base this approach not on the probability of a data processing disaster, but rather on the debilitating consequences of the loss of the function. If disaster recovery is presented to top management as a wise, cost-effective insurance plan—a program every bit as important as any policy the company manages—the recovery concept can stand on its own considerable merits.

Source: John Ratliff. Used by permission.

10.3 TURNING THEORY INTO REALITY

10.3.1 Identify and Set Priorities for Critical Applications

Identifying and setting priorities for critical applications will be the hardest tasks in the development of a disaster recovery plan. Two basic responses are common when a business manager is asked which systems are critical to the survival of the organization:
1. "All of my systems are critical; why else would I use them?"
2. "None are critical."
One manager once told me that he thought his operational efficiency and security would be improved if his small computer system was totally destroyed. This answer, however, is an extreme one and perhaps better represented his dislike of the system's inflexibility rather then the true disaster recovery needs of his department.

Neither "all" nor "none" can be acceptable. It is important to understand the types of systems that may be critical, and to apply a business rationale to the definitions of "survival" and "criticality."

The IBM Corporation at a DRP course suggested that businesses consider the following business criteria when determining criticality:[5]

- Safeguard company or organization assets
- Guard employee equities and rights
- Protect evidence of stockholder ownership
- Ensure capability to meet customer requirements
- Meet legal, regulatory or accounting requirements
- Help maintain competitive position
- Provide the user organization with its only way to carry out its primary responsibilities.

Setting priorities for the restoration applications can only be done after the systems have been identified and the consequences of their unavailability have been quantified. The factors to consider when setting priorities for critical systems are the duration of system unavailability, business cycle timing of the unavailability, and extent of the losses during the period of unavailability. The forms provided later in this chapter provide an easy method to collect the information required to identify and set priorities for critical application systems.

Systems that are not designated as critical systems may be classified as DISCRETIONARY and NONESSENTIAL. Discretionary systems are those systems that do not need to be restored to service immediately to ensure the survival of the organization; but they must be restored within some short period of time to keep the organization operational. An example of a discretionary system could be the organization's general ledger system. However, the specific determination as to which systems are discretionary rather than critical must be made on the basis of their impact on the organization.

Nonessential systems are those systems that can be put on the shelf for a while without significantly impacting the organization. Remember, we are talking about requirements to keep the company in business

---

[5]IBM Information Systems Management Institute, class discussion material, Chicago, IL, 12/83.

while it recovers from a disaster! Systems that have not yet been implemented are prime candidates for the nonessential designation; so are long-range reporting and forecasting applications.

10.3.2 Decide on an Alternate Processing Strategy

Knowing which systems are critical and what the processing requirements for those systems are will enable an organization to evaluate alternative processing availabilities for critical systems. These include:

1. Alternate Company Data Center

One solution to alternate processing availability is to provide internal data processing service capabilities at another company facility. This alternative is workable when:

    A. the same management controls both (all) data centers;

    B. sufficient processing and data communications capability is available to meet the critical workload requirements of both facilities as well as periodic disruption recovery testing;

    C. processing hardware, software, and communications compatibility are maintained.

The alternate company center approach can experience difficulties when:

    A. the same management cannot control both centers;

    B. disruptions are the result of widespread employee actions;

    C. two centers are in close physical proximity to each other.

2. Commercial Hotsite

Large data centers are available for use as disruption recovery facilities. They are equipped with computers and communications equipment which, contractually, are available to any subscriber who declares a disaster. The advantages of a hotsite facility include:

    A. rapid availability of a dedicated, professionally managed computer facility;

    B. technical support staff to assist in testing and recovery operations;

    C. consulting staff services availability.

The disadvantages of a commercial hotsite may include:

A. cost for a large scale service availability and testing which can exceed $100,000 per year;

B. cost to declare a disaster and activate the hotsite, as well as an ongoing daily usage charge;

C. capacity and special equipment limitations;

D. location convenience to the business operations.

3. Service Bureau

Commercial service bureaus, companies that offer processing services on a charge basis, can provide disruption recovery capabilities. This can be economically advantageous when:

A. the number of critical applications is small;

B. an existing relationship with the service bureau is in effect;

C. special equipment or supercomputer backup is required and it is available at the service bureau.

The disadvantages of using a service bureau can include:

A. cost;

B. capacity limitations;

C. data communications limitations.

4. Reciprocal Agreements

Reciprocal agreements may be formed between two independent organizations to provide backup processing service in the event of a disruption. One advantage of this can be that there is no charge for coverage.

Reciprocal agreements are a practical alternative when batch processing systems are involved and neither system has a heavy workload. There are, however, many disadvantages which include:

A. compatibility of hardware, software, and communications equipment;

B. maintaining compatibility of hardware, software, and communications equipment;

C. availability of sufficient processing and communications capacity when needed;

D. difficulty in enforcing a reciprocal agreement.

5. Coldsite

Environmentally conditioned computer rooms are available commercially and as part of some organizations' internal expansion plans. They are essentially empty computer rooms waiting to be equipped. The advantages of coldsites include:

A. operational readiness in one to two weeks;

B. lower cost than a hotsite.

The disadvantages include:

A. one- to two-week minimum before they are usable as a computer facility; communication equipment delays can prolong the wait before the coldsite can be used;

B. no ability to test recovery plan.

Note: Some hotsite facilities also offer coldsite facility coverage to supplement the hotsite facility service. This provides immediate service availability for short-term needs, and a transfer to a lower-cost facility for longer-range operations.

10.3.3 Develop the Plan

As stated earlier in this chapter, the disaster recovery plan must be more than a fat book in the data processing manager's bookcase. It must be integrated into the daily activities of the business.

The plan is really three plans in one. The first subplan is the EMERGENCY RESPONSE PLAN. Its purpose is to provide practical procedures for keeping minor crises, such as small fires and water leaks, from escalating into disasters. It should be readily available in the data center and be regularly used by operations personnel. The emergency plan may also be referred to as the DISRUPTION PLAN.

The second subplan is the BACKUP PLAN. Its purpose is to restore and maintain critical applications processing after a major disruption or a disaster has substantially reduced or destroyed data processing capabilities. The backup plan may also come to be known as the DISASTER PLAN.

The third subplan is the RESTORATION PLAN. Its purpose is to return operations to normalcy. This plan may include restoration of discretionary and nonessential processing, movement to an activated coldsite, or return to a rebuilt or new company data center.

The plan should be as simple as is practically possible. It should not be an exercise in writing prose for posterity. The emphasis of the plan should be on responsibility assignments, procedural checklists, and lists of requirements and contacts. The outline for developing a disaster recovery plan is included here. It has been organized as a checklist to help the reader to identify important issues in the plan development process.

THE DISASTER RECOVERY PLAN

I. EMERGENCY RESPONSE PLAN

A. INITIATION

1. Assumptions
Define emergency response definitions and rationale

2. Procedures
Define what to do for each type of emergency situation such as fire, water leak, employee injury.

3. Emergency Contacts
Include management contacts and phone numbers, as well as the message to be given to the person contacted.

B. CONCLUSION

1. Specify what is to be performed after the emergency response has been concluded. Include reports, supplies re-order, changes to procedures, and the like.

II. BACKUP PLAN

A. INITIATION

1. Assumptions
Define purpose of the plan, what is covered, what is not covered, definitions, and rationale.

2. Plan Activation
Define what circumstances will require plan activation and how to do it. Include appropriate emergency delegations of authority to authorize facility activation and other funding requirements.

3. Emergency Contacts
Include management and recovery team contacts and phone numbers that will reach higher into the organization than EMERGENCY RESPONSE contacts, and the message to be given to the person contacted.

4. Management Reporting
Include general guidance as to the progress reporting that will be required throughout the recovery and return to normal operations.

B. IMPLEMENTATION

The implementation section of the backup plan should contain the team responsibility and procedure checklists for effecting recovery operations. Each team leader should be responsible for the preparation and maintenance of his/her respective sections(s). The recovery teams may include:

–general management
–application system management
–data center management
–computer operations
–technical support (hardware/software)
–user services
–security
–vital records
–personnel
–logistics
–public relations
–support services
–plan testing
–plan updating

C. TEST PROCEDURES

1. Specify the frequency of plan testing.

2. Specify responsibilities for plan testing.

D. PLAN MAINTENANCE PROCEDURES

1. Specify who, how, and the frequency of plan maintenance.
2. Specify the type of testing to be performed.
3. Specify how plan maintenance is to be audited.

III. RESTORATION PLAN

A. INITIATION

1. Objectives

   Define what is to be accomplished during the restoration phase. This will include nonessential processing restoration, salvage operations, equipment reordering, facility rebuilding, and the like.

2. Procedures and Contacts

   Define who will be responsible for restoration activities. This must be coordinated with team designations described above, or separate restoration teams, similar to the backup teams, may be created.

B. IMPLEMENTATION

1. The restoration begins concurrently with the disaster recovery.

2. Implementation is completed when recovery is completed.

IV. APPENDIX

The appendix to the disaster recovery plan should contain the inventories that will be required during plan activation.

The inventories should include:

   A. Critical applications
   B. Vital records
   C. Data communications equipment
   D. Data processing equipment
   E. Software
   F. Supplies
   G. Logistics

A. CRITICAL APPLICATIONS

1. Define critical application criteria.

2. List each critical application with an application summary from the "Minimum Disaster Recovery Requirements Form." (See page 195.)

3. List the management contacts for each application system.

B. VITAL RECORDS INVENTORY

1. Define vital records criteria. Refer to organization policies and structures.

2. Specify scheduling procedures, vaulting procedures, and retrieval procedures.

3. Identify all vital records maintained for disruption recovery, their relationship to critical systems, specific scheduling, retention periods, storage locations.

4. Include procedures for re-creating damaged or destroyed records.

5. *Note:* The disaster recovery plan is a vital record. It should be included as part of the vital records program of the organization.

C. DATA COMMUNICATIONS EQUIPMENT INVENTORY

1. Include an inventory of all data communications equipment and software in use at the data center. Be specific as to the model and serial number. Indicate all upgrades to the equipment.

2. Include application system network charts at varying levels of detail as may be appropriate to the size and complexity of the data center.

3. Include vendor contacts and agreements for equipment and software replacement with estimated emergency replacement lead times.

4. Include scheduled plans for upgrading the network and communications equipment.

D. DATA PROCESSING EQUIPMENT INVENTORY

1. Include an inventory of all data processing equipment in use at the data center. Be specific as to the model and serial number. Indicate all upgrades to the equipment.

2. Include configuration charts at various levels of detail as may be appropriate to the size and complexity of the equipment.

3. Include vendor contacts and agreements for equipment replacement with estimated emergency replacement lead times.

4. Include scheduled plans for upgrading the equipment.

E. SOFTWARE INVENTORY

1. Include an inventory of all software that is supported by the data center. Be specific as to the version, release, change level, and so forth.

2. Include all authorizations and agreements to use the software at alternate processing sites for testing and recovery purposes.

3. Include vendor contacts and agreements for software replacement with estimated emergency replacement lead times. It should not be necessary to contact vendors if the vital records program is working properly, but be prepared for the worst.

4. Include scheduled plans for upgrading software.

5. *Note:* Check to be sure that the software inventory items are part of the vital records program.

F. SUPPLIES INVENTORY

1. Indicate all forms and supplies that are needed for critical and discretionary applications processing.

2. Indicate any staging areas used as part of the supply distribution system such as company and vendor warehouses. Similarly, include other locations within the organization that use the same forms and supplies.

3. Include vendor contacts and agreements for forms and supplies replacement with estimated emergency replacement lead times.

4. Include previous vendor/bidder contacts for forms and supplies.

5. Include the storage locations of any form master copies or plates that may be maintained at other than vendor locations.

G. LOGISTICS INVENTORY

1. Include an inventory of all company facilities that could be used as alternate data processing installations and the key management contacts at those locations.

2. Include a requirements definition for office facilities, equipment, and supplies that would be needed by disaster recovery and application user teams.

3. Include floor layout plans to be used at alternate processing facility locations. Be sure to review this with the alternate site host or vendor.

4. Include company contacts for logistics.

5. Include vendor contacts for lodging, food, and transportation at the alternate processing facility.

10.4 SAMPLE FORMS TO HELP GET STARTED

Defining and prioritizing those applications which are critical to the survival of your organization will be the most difficult task in developing and maintaining your disaster recovery contingency plan. The sample forms in this section will help you to develop data collection forms for identifying critical application systems and the processing requirements for those systems. The sample forms were provided by courtesy of the IBM Corporation's Information Systems

Management Institute, Chicago, Il. where they are used in conjunction with a disaster recovery planning class.[6] The specific forms included are:

1. I/S DISASTER RECOVERY REQUIREMENTS SIGNOFF

The "Signoff Form" is used to identify vital work products at the department level. A work product may be an application system such as a payroll system.

sample

```
             I/S DISASTER RECOVERY REQUIREMENTS SIGNOFF


Our   organization,  _____,  has
(please check one):


        _____ No vital work products that fit into the disaster
              recovery program for     I/S.


        _____ The following vital work products identified to
              I/S:  (Please list names and prioritize by importance
              with 1 as highest level.)
              a. Those required within 2 days:




              b. Those required within 2 weeks:




The requirements for     I/S disaster recovery are detailed on
the attached sheets.



SIGNED _____        PRINT NAME_____

DEPT/ZIP_____         PHONE     _____



Return this form and associated data by 1/15/80 to your User
Liaison contact:

        User Liaison
        R54/E16

                    CONFIDENTIAL WHEN FILLED IN
```

Copyright 1981 by International Business Machines Corporation. Reprinted by permission.

---

[6]IBM Information Systems Management Institute, Disaster Recovery Planning, "Determining Critical Applications," class discussion material, Chicago, Ill, 12/83, pp. 1, 17-25, and 27-29.

2. MINIMUM DISASTER RECOVERY REQUIREMENTS

The "Minimum Disaster Recovery Requirements Form" provides the means to record the hardware, software, and data necessary to recover an application.

```
              MINIMUM DISASTER RECOVERY REQUIREMENTS


VITAL WORK PRODUCT NAME _____

NAME _____    DATE _____

USER ORGANIZATION _____

1. Check reason this work product is considered vital (ref: RMS 10 01):
   __ Safeguarding company assets.
   __ Guarding employee equities and rights.
   __ Protecting evidence of stockholder ownership.
   __ Insuring        capability to meet custo.er commitments.

2. Complete Attachment 1 for services and time required.

3. Complete Attachment 2 for program products ·equired.  (Native
   requirements are not included here. These must be part of the
   using department's own vital record schedule and disaster
   recovery plan).

4. Complete Attachment 3 for hardware requirements needed to
   process this vital work product.

5. List all network nodes or locations you must exchange critical
   data with (both inside and external to     ):
```

```
6. List user departments whose vital records data fall under
   this vital work product:
```

```
7. Complete Attachment 4 for each department listed, providing a
   comphrensive list of data that must be reconstructed in event
   of a disaster.
```

3. EVALUATING THE IMPACT OF APPLICATION LOSS QUESTIONNAIRE

The "Questionnaire" permits the owner to easily record the key factors that will be necessary to evaluate the criticality of an application.

```
                    MINIMUM DISASTER REQUIREMENTS


Attachment 1

VITAL WORK PRODUCT (APPLICATION) NAME _____

Denote MINIMUM services required during a disaster situation
by completing the appropriate lines.
```

SERVICE REQUIRED	FREQ REQ'D *	TIME REQ'D **	SPECIAL CONSIDERATIONS ***	CURR SYS USED	NO OF USERS	MIP HRS/ MO
CMS						
CMS BATCH						
VM-EC						
TSO						
MVS BATCH						
VSPC						
DOS BATCH						
VS1 BATCH						
NETWORK ACCESS						
NATIVE						
APL						
OTHER, SPECIFY						

```
*    How often is service required--daily, weekly, monthly, twice week
**   Amount of time required within the frequency (30 min./day)
***  Include special scheduling (ex. 3rd shift), day of month, etc.
```

MINIMUM DISASTER REQUIREMENTS

Attachment 2

VITAL WORK PRODUCT (APPLICATION) NAME _____

Complete this form for each Program Product required in a disaster situation.

PROGRAM PRODUCT	VM	MVS
1. Compilers (Ex. PLS, FORTRAN)		
2. Utilities (Ex. SORT, Editors)		
3. Data Base Products (Ex. IMS, CICS)		
4. Library Management Products (Ex. CLEAR)		

MINIMUM DISASTER REQUIREMENTS

Attachment 2 Page 2

VITAL WORK PRODUCT (APPLICATION) NAME _____

PROGRAM PRODUCT	VM	MVS
5. FDP, IUP, Local Mods		
6. Other, specify		

MINIMUM DISASTER REQUIREMENTS

Attachment 3

VITAL WORK PRODUCT (APPLICATION) NAME _____

Complete form for <u>MINIMUM</u> hardware requirements — disaster
situation.

DEVICES	MODEL	QUANTITY	USAGE/WEEK IN HOURS	SPECIAL FEATURES
CPU (only for native or special CPU requirements)				
DISK DRIVES				
TAPE DRIVES				
TERMINALS				

MINIMUM DISASTER REQUIREMENTS

Attachment 3 Page 2

VITAL WORK PRODUCT (APPLICATION) NAME _____

DEVICES	MODEL	QUANTITY	USAGE/WEEK IN HOURS	SPECIAL FEATURES
KEYPUNCH				
MSS				
PRINTER				
T.P. EQUIP.				
OTHER (include special devices)				

MINIMUM DISASTER RECOVERY REQUIREMENTS

Attachment 4

VITAL WORK PRODUCT (APPLICATION) NAME _____

DEPARTMENT NUMBER/NAME _____

Data required to process during disaster situation:

1. Insure permanently mounted user disk packs required are on
    the copy of your department's   Vital Records Schedule
    (ZM03-7981-03) kept by   DP Storage Administration,
    R56/E17   List which ones you will require for this
    vital work product.

2. Off-line media (disk packs, tapes, MSS cartridges)
    required in disaster situation must be part of your
    department's vital records schedule and handled by
    individual requests at the tape/disk library for media to
    be sent to vital records. Insure this is done and current
    or your vital data will not be available.

3. VM User ID's Required (include mini-disks owned by your
    user ID as well as mini-disks you link to but do not own.
    To determine your virtual address issue the command 'CP
    QUERY VIRTUAL DASD'):

USER ID	VIRTUAL ADDRESSES	CURRENT SYSTEM	DEPT, IF DIFFERENT

MINIMUM DISASTER RECOVERY REQUIREMENTS

Attachment 4 Page 2

VITAL WORK PRODUCT (APPLICATION) NAME _____

DEPARTMENT NUMBER/NAME _____

4. List   TSO User ID's and special logon requirements:

5. MVS   - List critical on-line data set names required
    for this vital product. (Insure all datasets are included
    for JCL, programs, libraries, data, procs.)

EVALUATING THE IMPACT OF APPLICATION LOSS

The primary purpose of this questionnaire is to assist the <u>application owner</u> to make some business judgments. These business judgments have to do with the organizational impact of the loss of the application.

The questionnaire is meant to be used as a discussion vehicle for the owner and the disaster recovery planner.

It can be used also to help senior executives to think through what are the most critical business functions and the applications that support them.

_____
                    APPLICATION NAME
Use a separate form for each application.

1. Organizational impact: the loss of this application would have the following effect on the organization:

    __ A. Catastrophic effect on the organization or some
          divisions

    __ B. Catastrophic effect on one to three divisions

    __ C. Moderate effect on the organization

    __ D. Moderate effect on one to three divisions

    __ E. Minor effect on the organization or some divisions

2. How long can your department continue to perform all of its functions without usual data processing support? Assume that loss of data processing support has occurred during your busiest or peak period. Check one only.

    __ Up to three days

    __ Up to one week

    __ Up to one month

    __ Other. Please specify _____

3. Indicate a peak time of the year, and or a peak day of the week, if any, for this application.

J F M A M J J A S O N D

S M T W T F S

Any other peak load considerations: _____

_____

4. Have you developed/established any back-up procedures (manual or otherwise) which can be used to continue operations in the event that this application is unavailable?

__ Yes   __ No

If Yes, have the procedures been tested?

__ Yes, within the last six months.

__ Yes, in the past year.

__ Yes, but over a year ago.

__ No.

Use these codes for the
  next three questions.

A - over $10,000,000
B - $1,000,000 - $10,000,000
C - $100,000 - $1,000,000
D - $10,000 - $100,000
E - up to $10,000

5. The loss of this application would result in lost revenue from fees, collections, interest penalties, ...:

__ Day 1
__ Day 2
__ Day 4
__ Week 1
__ Month 1

6. The loss of this application would erode our customer base over a period of time. The cost to the organization from lost business would be:

__ Day 3
__ Week 1
__ Week 2
__ Week 3
__ Month 1

7. The loss of this application would result in the
   following fines and penalties due to regulatory
   requirements (Federal, state, local...):

   __ Day 1
   __ Day 2
   __ Day 4
   __ Week 1
   __ Month 1

8. The loss of this application would have legal ramifications due to regulatory
   statutes, contractual agreements, etc. Specify potential areas of exposure:

   _____

   _____

9. The loss of this application would have the following negative impact on the
   people for whom you are responsible:

   _____

   _____

10. The loss of this application would keep us from supplying services to out-
    side customers. Specify:

    _____

    _____

11. Specify any other factors which should be considered in evaluating the im-
    pact of the loss of this application.

    _____

    _____

chapter 11
Dealing with Special Personnel Considerations

This chapter addresses two difficult management tasks: terminating the services of EDP employees and supervising computer security officers and EDP auditors. It will help the manager to avoid the "you didn't tell me" responses that are so prevalent in computer-related problem situations.

Use the suggestions in this chapter to help you to maintain an open and up-front relationship of individual trust, responsibility, and accountability. That relationship starts with clearly advising each employee what is expected of him at the time of employment, continues with training and supervision, and concludes when the individual leaves the organization.

11.1 TERMINATING THE SERVICES OF EDP EMPLOYEES

Terminating the services of any employee is an extremely unpleasant management responsibility. A checklist of procedures to follow will not make you feel any better. It will, however, help you to make sure that you protect the rights of the individual and the assets of the organization. This section will help you determine if your organization protects its assets in a satisfactory manner when terminating the services of an EDP employee, and will assist you in preparing a checklist of actions to be followed during the termination process.

11.1.1 Laying the Foundation

Termination procedures begin at the time of hire. At a minimum, every new EDP employee should be given a copy of the organization's policy that specifies the authorized use of data and processing resources (see Chapter Eight) and must be required to acknowledge this receipt in writing. The policy must be provided to each employee so that the employee understands what is expected with regard to the security of the organization's assets. It also provides the legal basis for administrative, civil, and criminal actions if the employee fails to comply with the policy.

The policy must be supplemented by signed acknowledgments for all equipment for which the employee is to be held personally responsible for returning, such as vehicles, portable computers, keys, ID cards, and parking permits. Confidentiality and nondisclosure agreements, where appropriate, should also be signed at the time of employment.

Consider this scenario to put the need for acknowledged employment documents in perspective. Your auditor has found a considerable volume of non-company data and numerous programs to process this data on an employee's disk storage space. You conclude that the employee may be operating a private business on your company's computer. You question the employee and obtain an admission of guilt. The employee also tells you something that you did not expect— that you never told the employee that she could not use the computer for personal work, and it didn't cost the organization anything because the computer wasn't busy anyway.

I was surprised when I heard the "you never told me" statement for the first time. It was restated by more people during other investigations that I conducted. So, I must conclude that it is not obvious to all employees that it is wrong, and perhaps illegal in some jurisdictions, to use an employer's computer to conduct personal or non-company business activity without prior approval. It is better to notify employees in advance of your policy regarding the personal use of the organization's computer; whether or not such use is acceptable. Don't wait until a situation arises where the legality of unauthorized use must be resolved.

11.1.2 Terminations for Cause

Data processing employees must be discharged in a manner consistent with the release of any employee who has considerable access to the organization's critical information and tangible assets. A disgruntled or vindictive employee who mishandles physical assets is easy to notice and can be removed from situations where more harm can be done. The early detection and removal of a disgruntled or vindictive EDP employee is not always possible.

Lengthy termination procedures can provide an employee with ample opportunities to test your computer security procedures and to initiate changes that will cause damage at some future date. Computer programmers present the greatest risk potential because they are authorized to modify computer programs; but every employee with the ability to access and modify computer programs and data is a security risk.

Incidents that clearly violate criminal statutes, such as the theft or diversion of organization assets, are obvious grounds for dismissal, and they are the easiest to deal with, even where union contracts or civil service regulations require lengthy termination procedures. Policy violations are more difficult to handle.

Consider this approach when you believe that the services of an employee must be terminated for cause:

1. Be very sure of your facts and your organization's procedures before you confront the employee, especially where computer-related fraud and abuse are involved. You will need help to be certain that your evidence is collected and evaluated properly.

2. Keep your management advised of all relevant progress in an investigation that may result in the dismissal of an employee.

3. Check with your legal and personnel departments to be sure that your grounds for dismissal and substantiating documentation are sufficient and that you are acting in accordance with company policy.

4. Advise your management that you will dismiss or suspend the employee on an immediate basis. You may be required to suspend the employee with pay until the employee has exhausted all procedural remedies. Be prepared to convince your management that salary costs are cheaper than your potential losses if the employee were to become vindictive.

5. Request that a security person be present at the time scheduled for employee confrontation and dismissal if you believe that this is necessary.

6. Request that the employee come to your office.

7. Advise the employee of your evidence and evaluate any response or explanation that you are given.

8. Dismiss the employee immediately if an admission of guilt is offered, or suspend the employee, with or without pay, if that is more appropriate.

9. Demand the immediate return of all organization property and identification cards that may be in the employee's possession. Make arrangements for the return of any material that is not immediately available.

10. Request that the employee specify all computer processing accounts that he has used.

11. Advise the individual that he may no longer access the company's data and processing resources. Obtain a written acknowledgment from the individual or note that the person was advised on your termination form.

12. Have the individual escorted to his work area by an appropriate supervisor and have him remove all personal effects.

13. Change all computer access codes that the individual has acknowledged using or that you believe that he may have known.

14. Escort the individual from the organization's premises and make provisions for his safe transportation home.

15. Resolve the remaining procedural issues as is appropriate in your organization.

16. Thoroughly review the data and programs that the individual has had access to; also check the backup copies of these data and programs.

11.1.3 Terminations for Business Reasons

Layoffs, or reductions in force (RIF), of information systems personnel may be necessary. After you have determined which employees must be separated, dismiss them on an "immediate" basis with payment for any separation obligation, rather than require them to work for a few more days or weeks.

From a security viewpoint, immediate separation is beneficial to the organization because:

1. Normal disciplinary controls may not be effective. Employees may feel that they have nothing to lose. Supervisors may be reluctant to take appropriate disciplinary actions that they believe may be futile.
2. Resentment towards the organization by the laid-off employee may be spread to other employees.
3. Vindictive actions by the laid-off employee may result in lost or misfiled data, programs, and documentation.
4. Trojan horses, logic time bombs imbedded in computer programs, and other unauthorized data or program modifications may be made by the laid-off employee that will not be discovered until some future date.

From a personal viewpoint, you and the employee will benefit from a paid immediate separation. The immediate termination of employment minimizes the employee's period of agony and embarrassment, and provides the employee with a full-time opportunity to find a new position. It also reduces the period of embarrassment or uneasiness that will be felt by those employees who will not be separated. Therefore, for both security and positive management reasons, end all employee separations as quickly as possible.

11.2 PROBATIONARY PERIODS

Employee probationary periods create an increased period of stress for both an employee and management. Your intent may be to give the employee a fair opportunity to demonstrate that improved performance or attitude is possible. The employee may view it as a procedure that management must follow prior to her ultimate dismissal.

You, as the probationer's manager, must carefully balance the need to provide a fair opportunity for the employee to demonstrate a return to a satisfactory performance level, ongoing departmental productivity requirements, and an increased need to protect the organization's assets. Whatever your personal feelings towards the individuals are, you must think of the probationary period in the most basic of terms. Would you allow a person with financial responsibilities to continue to write checks for the organization? Would you allow a secretary who was on probation to continue to type, sign, and mail your confidential correspondence? Probably not.

The probationary employee may share your desire to demonstrate improved performance and retain her job by dramatically changing the quality and quantity of work output. However, this increased productivity may realistically result in an increased error rate that may not be immediately detectable, particularly where complex computer programming is involved. Also, at some point during the probationary period, the employee may begin to believe that she has no possibility of retaining her job, and decide to take some vindictive action that will remind the organization of its unfairness. It is your responsibility to deal effectively with these potential security risks before they cause problems.

Here are some suggestions for preventing computer security risks during probationary periods:

Prior to placing the employee on probation

1. Advise your computer security officer (CSO) of the planned action, and request that the CSO prepare a report of all data/program access capabilities of the employee.

2. Review the possibility of a task or project reassignment, within the scope of the terms and conditions of your organization's probation policies, if there is a real potential for data, program, or operational damage were the employee to become vindictive. Extra precautions should be taken regarding systems programmers who are on probation.

3. Copy any critical data and programs that the individual is responsible for, *or* extend the scratch or release date of previous backup tape copies of disks/tapes that contain the employee's work-related data and programs. The backups can, if required in the future, serve two purposes. They can be used to restore

operational data and programs. The backups may also be necessary if you are required to prove that unauthorized changes were made by the employee during the probationary period.

4. Restrict the employee's access capabilities to any data or programs that she will not need to use during the probationary period. This procedure is referred to as "logical access control." It is normally accomplished with the use of access control software and by changing passwords.

5. Restrict the employee's access to work areas by task or project reassignment. This is referred to as "physical access control" and may require a badge or key change.

During the Probationary Period

1. Advise the employee that she is being placed on probation and present the terms and conditions of the probation; include any work assignment modifications and access (logical and physical) restrictions.

2. Do not permit any unsupervised access to magnetic media libraries. Computer programmers and systems analysts are not normally permitted in these libraries. Librarians who are placed on probation must never be allowed to work alone in the library.

3. Do not permit unsupervised operation of computers by probationary computer operators.

4. Take unannounced computer "snapshot" copies of the probationary programmer's computer libraries and system work areas, if this is not precluded by your organization or legal statutes. Review them for authorized and unauthorized changes.

5. End the probationary period as quickly as possible. Restore the employee to regular work status or use the immediate termination procedure described above.

11.3 SUPERVISING COMPUTER SECURITY OFFICERS AND EDP AUDITORS

Computer Security Officer and EDP auditor supervision and control have been included because people in these positions are at times authorized to have access to otherwise restricted information, programs, and procedures within a data center; and because we believe that data center management has an affirmative obligation to "audit the auditors" with respect to any actions that Computer Security Officers and EDP auditors may take that could compromise data center security.

In theory, the same requirements for control should be present for Computer Security Officers and EDP auditors as they are for every other employee. In practice, however, it is not quite so simple because these are the people who develop, enforce, and review the controls for the organization.

11.3.1 Computer Security Officer Supervision

The most difficult Computer Security Officer to supervise and control, from a security viewpoint, is the Computer Security Officer who works within a data center reporting structure. She normally has an operational requirement for access to all, or most, data, programs, and documentation that you are responsible for processing and protecting. The Computer Security Officer may also have the ability and authority to make changes to these assets with or without your knowledge. Corporate level Computer Service Officers present less of a security risk because they do not usually have operational access capabilities. You, as the Computer Security Officer's manager, must hold the Computer Security Officer responsible for complying with the same rules of the organization as all other employees, and add those special requirements that are applicable to the position's responsibilities as you have defined them. The following suggestions are offered to help you with the special requirements.

1. Define Principal Responsibilities

The Computer Security Officer's principal responsibilities must be defined in a manner that is relevant to your operational requirements. They may be specified in much greater detail than those which your organization's personnel department needs to classify the position and may include:

- Supervise computer security staff
- Establish security policies and procedures
- Perform or coordinate EDP risk and vulnerability assessments

- Participate in application system development and review
- Administer computer log-on passwords
- Administer data access control systems
- Prepare security improvement recommendations
- Purchase and implement security systems and services
- Conduct security awareness meetings
- Provide security consulting expertise throughout the organization
- Coordinate all EDP audit activities
- Conduct computer abuse investigations
- Review activities of EDP auditors and systems programmers
- Supervise data center guard force

2. Recruit the Right Person

Recruit the right person for your organization. A large organization will require a computer security manager who has both management and computer security experience and skills, and a staff of other Computer Security Officers with varying degrees of managerial and technical abilities.

A small data center, or a division of a large company, may need only one individual to administer its security program. That person must then have a higher level of technical expertise than a large organization's Computer Security Officer, and as a minimum, good interpersonal skills.

Perform a background investigation for all computer security personnel. Computer security personnel must have a clean criminal history record. Former felons should not be employed unless they have very clearly demonstrated a successful return to society. Any misdemeanor offenses must be carefully evaluated. Hiring former law enforcement personnel can ease your burden of background checking in this area.

Check employment records. Computer Security Officers should have a demonstrated record of employment accomplishments. You may wish to develop your own Computer Security Officer or hire an experienced practitioner. Positive accomplishments are indicative of a good work attitude and proven abilities. Both are required.

Make it very clear to the person you plan to select as a Computer Security Officer that a high level of trust and confidentiality are conditions of continued employment. A less-than-honest Computer Security Officer is a much greater security risk to your organization than a less-than-effective Computer Security Officer. Hire accordingly.

3. Define What You Expect

Tell your Computer Security Officer what you want accomplished, what the Computer Security Officer's authority is, and the general and specific requirements and resources of the position. You and the Computer Security Officer are most vulnerable to improper actions of the Computer Security Officer. You can avoid problems when you establish an appropriate delineation of authority and a good reporting methodology.

Make sure that both you and the Computer Security Officer understand what is to happen when any of the following situations occur:

- security breaches
- major security vulnerabilities are detected
- investigations are in progress
- confidential data is examined
- unusual incidents are discovered
- the Computer Security Officer needs you immediately

4. Define Information Access Privileges

You must define or consent to the types of information that the Computer Security Officer may access, and under which circumstances the Computer Security Officer may access it. As a guideline, consider these access classifications:

Routinely Available

- passwords (log-on and data access)
- nonsecured data and text
- computer system performance and accounting records
- security log data
- file management data

- computer processing utilization data
- employee time records

Special Circumstance Availability

Situations may arise when the Computer Security Officer must examine data that is confidential or has been secured by its owner. It would be reasonable to expect a Computer Security Officer to access this data in the event of a security system failure, if there was reasonable cause to suspect a security breach, or during a computer abuse investigation. The conditions under which a special circumstance may permit Computer Security Officer access to otherwise secured information must be defined, and appropriate controls established.

On Request Availability

The effectiveness of a Computer Security Officer, in part, depends on access to data center information that is normally considered privileged. Primarily, this will involve information about staff members. You may wish to routinely advise your Computer Security Officer of pending staff situations such as reorganization plans, promotions, demotions, and dismissals. This would be appropriate in large organizations where the Computer Security Officer is a manager with significant operational responsibilities.

Computer Security Officers who are primarily technicians, as they would be in smaller organizations, may only need to know of pending personnel actions at the time that they are to take place so that data access privileges can be revoked. Balancing the Computer Security Officer's access to confidential information should be a function of position requirements, need to know, and demonstrated security professionalism.

5. Make Yourself Available for Informal Meetings

A Computer Security Officer must be able to "brainstorm" or discuss ideas and problem-solving strategies in an informal manner with her manager. Computer security is a new and specialized field that you may not technically understand. At a minimum, you should serve as a sounding board. More likely, you can provide an overview on the impact of any proposed major changes and business reasons why strategies may or may not be effective.

6. Follow Up Complaints About the Computer Security Officer

You may expect to receive complaints about any employee who has a control function. Complaints about Computer Security Officers that involve actions relating to data access control will probably occur whenever new restrictions are imposed. Too many (the number is hard to define) complaints of this nature may mean poor planning by the Computer Security Officer. Too many complaints may also be an indicator of an abuse or misunderstanding of authority. Follow up appropriately.

Complaints about the lack of diplomacy of the Computer Security Officer should rarely occur. These may indicate a personality clash, or another, perhaps unrelated, security issue that will require your attention.

Complaints about any unauthorized data access will require priority action by you, and perhaps skilled technicians. An investigation may have been compromised or the Computer Security Officer may have exceeded her authority. Either situation must be resolved very quickly.

7. Review Computer Access Actions

You, or possibly an EDP auditor, should periodically review the actions performed by the Computer Security Officer that involve computer resource utilization or data accesses. Data accesses that involve "special circumstance availability" can only be considered as appropriately controlled if you conduct these reviews.

11.3.2 EDP Auditor Supervision

The EDP auditor must work within the policies and guidelines of the organization and should be directly supervised by his manager. The audit department's charter may include the right to request any documents, data, programs, and individual employee knowledge relevant to an approved audit. The audit department should not be allowed to have uncontrolled access to any materials that have been classified for restricted use.

The area where conflicts may arise involves attempts to access resources or data that have not been approved in advance as part of the audit. You, as the manager who becomes aware of any unauthorized activity in your area of responsibility, have an obligation to determine what has been attempted, and to take appropriate actions. This requires that you supervise and control selected activities of EDP auditors. It does not mean or imply that you have any right whatsoever to attempt to gain access to any unauthorized audit materials.

A further clarification of these responsibilities may be necessary. Auditors must have complete access to all materials relevant to any audit that has been appropriately approved. They have an expectation of absolute privacy regarding their work papers, data, and computer programs. They should not have an expectation of privacy with regard to the areas that they physically visit, the names of the computer programs and data files that they access, or the computational resources that they utilize.

As an example, if an auditor were assigned an office in your data center, it would be reasonable for you to log and review by date and time each entry and exit to the data center. This would normally be done for all employees with the reports provided by your physical access control system. It would be unacceptable, however, for you or your staff to attempt to gain access to the materials contained within the auditor's office, desk, or file cabinets.

The example also applies to auditor data processing activities. It would be reasonable and prudent for your Computer Security Officer to review the computer accounting records of EDP auditors to determine if access was attempted or accomplished for any restricted programs or data that had not been authorized to the auditors. It would also be necessary to determine if someone masquerading as an EDP auditor had attempted to compromise your security. This is what Computer Security Officers normally do.

A documented, unauthorized, computer-related activity by an EDP auditor should be investigated by the Computer Security Officer as if it were a security violation by any other computer system user. The investigation would, or would not, include the audit department in accordance with the security procedures of the organization and the employee(s) who was involved. Investigative procedures are provided in Chapter Nine.

You or your organization's management may not agree with this auditor control philosophy. Review the following summary suggestions with the appropriate department(s) in your organization before acting on them.

1. Restrict Physical Access

Restrict the access of EDP auditors to work areas that are related to specific audit activities. They should not be allowed into any areas of the data center that are not authorized in advance. Access control is easiest to administer with the same procedures or devices, such as access badge readers, that all employees are required to use.

2. Require Formal Requests for Logical Access

Do not permit EDP auditors to have computer access to any data or programs that are protected by logical access control software without an approved written request. Accepting verbal requests for access to restricted use materials (data, programs, or documentation) can result in your being cited for poor control procedures.

The approval for access authorization must be developed for your organization. It may be sufficient for the audit manager to sign the request. It would be more appropriate for both the audit manager and the owner of the data or programs to sign the request.

The procedures that you develop for permitting logical access to restricted use materials during the conduct of a computer-related abuse investigation may be different from access approval requirements during an audit. An investigator who may be an EDP auditor, Computer Security Officer, or law enforcement official, may be granted unrestricted access to any or all materials that may be needed during an investigation.

You have an obligation to cooperate and comply with requests made during the investigation if the request is appropriately approved by your management. However, you place yourself in personal jeopardy if the request is not substantiated by written authorization and each access is not substantiated by a log of events.

3. Review All Data and Program Access Attempts

Review the accounting and security reports produced by your computer. Look for attempts by EDP auditors to gain access to restricted data or programs that have not been authorized in advance.

Unauthorized attempts, by any EDP auditor, to access restricted data or programs may indicate that:

1. A confidential investigation is in progress. This should not occur if there is proper coordination between data center and audit personnel.
2. EDP audit is surreptitiously testing your access control security. This may or may not be an acceptable technique in your organization.
3. An EDP auditor made an honest mistake. This should rarely occur.
4. A real security incident has occurred. An EDP auditor or someone masquerading as an EDP auditor has attempted to compromise your security.

chapter 12
Dealing with Microcomputer Security

This chapter brings controls and security measures for small computers into the same perspective as those for large computers. It recommends methods for handling those security opportunities that are specific to microcomputers.

As you read this chapter, keep in mind that the value of the information that is stored and processed by a microcomputer may not have any relationship whatsoever to the low cost of the equipment. Base your protective measures on the impact of the losses that could result from system compromises in the same manner that you would if a large computer were being used.

12.1 UNDERSTANDING A MICROCOMPUTER

Microcomputers, which are also known as personal computers (PCs), and word processing systems will impact the security of your office operations. You can directly control the security of microcomputers that are used only in your office. Micros that are connected to other computers require additional security measures that are discussed in Chapters Two and Four.

A microcomputer is a small, perhaps even portable, computer. Considerable effort has been expended trying to classify small computers in terms of processing speed, main memory size, data storage capacity, and cost. Constantly improving technology has resulted in, and will continue to result in, the development of small computers that significantly surpass the processing and data storage capabilities of models produced only a few years earlier. Therefore, it is easiest just to think of a microcomputer as a small computer that uses the same technical concepts as a large computer.

A business microcomputer is an electronic device with processing capability, main memory, and substantial auxiliary data storage capacity. Main memory is where the program in use resides together with the data or text that is being processed.

The size of a unit's main memory is measured in characters (BYTES). The minimum storage capacity needed for micro business applications is 64K, or 64,000 bytes. Expect to see this minimum requirement increase as technology advances and more complex programs are developed. One Meg, or million character, main memory machines are becoming available.

Data, text, and programs that are not actively in use are kept in auxiliary or secondary storage. The media most commonly used for auxiliary storage are disks and smaller disks, also known as diskettes. The unit that controls access to the disk is a disk drive. It may be contained within the micro or may be a separate unit plugged into the micro.

A micro may be used to process data or text. Most can do both. Software (computer programs) controls whether the micro is performing as a computer or as a text (word) processor.

A micro, or larger than micro minicomputer, may better meet your business needs than buying time on your organization's large computer system. This is especially true if you are tired of waiting for the computer department to solve your information problem with an elegant, and perhaps expensive, solution that an outside vendor can demonstrate as immediately solvable by even a beginner and a micro.

Your introduction of a microcomputer into your operations brings with it computer security responsibilities. The primary areas of concern will be data security and the physical security of the micro. They require special consideration and attention because most business managers have not previously had to deal with computer security issues, and because both the microcomputer system and its data can be very easily damaged, lost, or stolen.

12.2 PROTECTING THE MICROCOMPUTER

Data security is the most important concern to be addressed in protecting microcomputers. Part of the problem is that a micro seems so similar to a large computer terminal that links the user to a professionally protected large computer, and because micro operation usually requires the operator to have physical access to the computer, programs, and data. Let's look at the similarities and differences, because you can make your micro almost as secure as a large computer system with a reasonable level of direct expense.

The design philosophy of a micro is very different from that of a large computer. A micro is designed to be operated by almost anyone. If you can turn a micro on and read displayed instructions, you can probably use the micro to process or retrieve information stored in it. Consider micro data security design issues in the context of large system access control security, specifically log-on access, data access, and data storage protection.

Large computer systems are designed for multiple concurrent use by many people. Log-on access control is the first level of security. The most common means to control large system log-on access is to require that a user have a previously authorized processing account and know a secret password to gain access to the computer. Contrast this with microcomputer log-on security.

Microcomputer log-on security rarely exists. The micro equivalent of a large computer terminal session is initiated by turning on the CPU. The software in the micro then presents a menu of system actions that can be initiated, as well as a "help" facility to guide the user along. This user friendly approach is necessary for micros because they are designed for easy use rather than for use only by technically trained staff members.

The micro session itself is also easy. A menu is used to select the data or text to be processed. The menu may provide a listing of programs and the data available on auxiliary storage. This is an important convenience factor for the business user, but you may require additional security measures to protect your information.

Selecting a micro application processing program, including text processing, from the menu may only require moving a cursor key and pushing a button. The programs and data are then obtained from internal disk storage or a request to insert a diskette is made by the micro. The diskette, if required, is probably located in a file box near the micro and should be clearly labeled. Insert it and you are ready to proceed.

Several security differences between a micro and a large computer system should be apparent. Let's review them in more detail.

In larger system application processing, the ability of a logged-on user to initiate processing of data could be controlled by limiting the ability of the user to know which application programs could be processed. This is normally accomplished by the computer allowing only certain terminals to be used for application processing, restricting application menus to authorized users, and restricting application processing capabilities, without a menu, to authorized users. Micro systems are not usually security-protected in this manner because they are not designed for security. They are designed to help the user get a job done with a minimum of data processing knowledge.

The second critical micro data security issue is related to the user's ability to physically have access to data. Larger computer operations normally have data stored on-line or in a media storage library. Authorization to use on-line or library data can be enforced with access control software and restrictions that prevent the user from being able to physically touch media that contain data. Micro logical access control software is not widely available and the physical insertion requirement of diskettes is both common and necessary.

Because diskettes must be available in or near microcomputers, it is especially important to consider the physical security of the data in your office. Memos and reports that are sensitive and confidential are usually stamped to indicate restrictive use. Procedures for transmitting and storing confidential information are routine and you know how to enforce them. Now look around your office or your secretary's office for the diskettes that were used to produce restricted access memos or reports. The diskettes are probably on top of the desk near the micro in an unlocked box or in a loose-leaf binder. The box or binder may or may not get put away or be secured during lunch hour or at the end of the day.

It is also highly probable that the diskettes contain a mix of confidential and unrestricted memos, and that no confidentiality markings have been applied to the diskettes. If this is a correct description of diskette storage in your office, you will need to address microcomputer data security as a high-priority item.

The examples above describe the most common problems of securing data in an otherwise well-run office. Don't overlook people-related environmental concerns in the office. Microcomputers and their diskettes are more susceptible to physical damage than larger computers because of their proximity to people.

A popular poster during the 1960s was the "deadly doughnut." It displayed a doughnut and a container of coffee near a computer tape and explained how easily either could damage the data contained on the magnetic computer tape. The same problem exists for microcomputers and data storage media such as diskettes and tape cassettes.

Perform an environmental impact analysis to see if your office conditions jeopardize your micro and data.

12.2.1 How to Evaluate the Office Environment

1. Check Media Vulnerability

Diskettes and tapes are extremely sensitive to damage that may result from static electricity, heat, direct sunlight, spilled beverages, dust, and cigarette smoke and ashes. Look around the area in which your diskettes and tapes are used and stored and you can readily determine if your data is vulnerable to damage.

2. Check Micro Vulnerability

The micro itself is susceptible to the same damage vulnerabilities as its data storage media. It may also be physically damaged by being dropped or banged when being moved.

3. Check for Clean Power

It is not uncommon to find micros using the same circuits as typewriters, fluorescent lights and refrigerators that add electrical interference and power surges (spikes). Fluctuating voltage levels pose a real problem for micros. Large computers eliminate this potential problem with expensive power smoothing devices. Similar care and expense is not routine for micros. The immediate result of this problem can be errors and the loss of data.

4. Check the Micro's Other Work and Storage Locations

Data security problems are increased when a micro or diskettes are taken to a client location or brought home. The valuable micro may be lost, stolen, or damaged in transit. It's a very practical concern and I personally think about it each time my micro rides in the trunk or on the back seat of my car.

Diskettes are equally vulnerable to loss and damage when taken out of the office. They can be easily damaged by heat, sunlight, and rain or snow. They should always be well protected while in transit.

12.2.2 Improvements to Make

Microcomputer security is easy to effect once you accept it as a personal responsibility. Don't wait for your organization to issue policies and guidelines. If they are not available, develop them for your area of responsibility by applying the information security standards of your organization and making the following improvements.

1. Specify Your Security Requirements

- Make it very clear that every employee who uses a microcomputer is responsible for the protection of the data, programs, and the microcomputer assigned to or used by him. This requires the separation of restricted use material from other office information. It also means physically locking up sensitive information.

  Encrypting data is a supplemental safeguard to physical data protection. But it is rarely used on large commercial computers and it is unreasonable to expect that easy-to-use encryption products for microcomputers, although currently available, will be in demand in the near future.

- Prohibit the unauthorized copying and use of the organization's data, which may include memos or reports as well as computer data files. This is a particular concern with microcomputers because the data is extremely compact, reproducible without any record of the copy being made, and the data is commonly carried from location to location.

- Prohibit the unauthorized copying and distribution of copyrighted programs and program documentation. Software piracy is a major problem for program developers. Permitting your employees to steal this material exposes you and your organization to needless legal liability.

- Define who (and for what reasons) may take a microcomputer and its data home or to another location; and how they are to be protected at off-site locations.

- Apply the same network security principles to microcomputers that are left on in a communications mode as are specified for mainframe computers.

2. Educate Your Staff About Micro Security

- Start by explaining why microcomputer security is important, and then go into specific protective measures that you think are necessary and reasonable. Don't forget to include your secretarial and word processing personnel in these discussions.

- Encourage the micro users to thoroughly understand the equipment, data, and programs that they are using.

3. Create a Proper Work Environment

- Provide your staff with appropriate office space and equipment for the micro and its accessories. This will include securely lockable storage space for diskettes.

- Provide electrical safeguards for the micro. These will include line surge protectors for the micro and its peripheral equipment. Static discharge floor pads should be used when micros are used in carpeted office areas.

4. Protect Diskettes

- Lock up diskettes when they are not in use. This is the cheapest, surest form of data security available for microcomputers.

- Mark diskettes according to the information security classification guidelines of your organization. Diskettes that contain confidential data or reports should be identified and handled accordingly.

- Make backup copies of diskettes. Diskettes are vulnerable to data loss and physical damage. Regular backup copies must be prepared of all critical information. The backups should be stored in a secured area away from the micro.

- Clearly index and file diskettes. This will save time as well as improve security.

- Erase diskettes that contain obsolete or unnecessary data. This reduces the number of obsolete copies of data that are being maintained and prevents mix-ups of restricted use information. They are erased by using a special utility program that overwrites the entire disk. The "erase" command does not really erase data.

5. Secure the Micro

- Secure the micro to its work station or make sure that the work area security is adequate to protect against equipment theft. Special anchoring devices are available that provide a high degree of tamper resistance and that also enable easy removal of the micro for servicing or use elsewhere.

6. Protect the Micro's Internal Data Storage

- Clear your micro's main memory before you allow someone else to use it. The micro may contain a copy of the last document or data that you were working on. Push the reset button, function key or turn the equipment off to clear the main memory.

- Don't allow other personnel to use your micro if it contains restricted use information in its internal memory, if the information is not protected by password, encryption, or other security systems. The internal memory may be hard disk, bubble memory, or some other form of auxiliary storage.

- Clear or overwrite the entire contents of all internal data storage devices before transferring or disposing of the micro; this also applies to memory typewriters. The State Department was embarrassed in 1984 when it failed to do this. Its highly sensitive information was discovered in a prison system that had received memory typewriters that had not been properly cleared.

7. Keep the Micro in Good Repair

- Clean the disk heads according to the manufacturer's schedule. The heads become dirty because of oxide accumulations on diskettes, cigarette smoke, dust, and other airborne contaminants. Dirty heads will result in lost data. Very little other service should be required for the micro.

8. Destroy Printer Ribbons

- Destroy all single strike ribbons that have been used to print sensitive information.

9. Check Your Insurance Policy

- Make sure that your insurance policy covers your micro when it is taken from your premises. Homeowner's insurance policies do not usually cover business equipment without a special rider.

12.3 WHY MICROCOMPUTERS WILL CHANGE YOUR RELATIONSHIP WITH EDP

The practicality of using microcomputers for some business applications, as well as the easy use and availability of microcomputers, is changing the present relationship between data processing managers and user managements. The impact of the microcomputer revolution will increase as microcomputers continue to become more powerful with growing data storage and communications capabilities.

There are many specific reasons why data processing managers have opposed the introduction of micros. The reasons may be classified into three broad areas of concern:

- Loss of EDP department control
- Impact on organizational data systems
- Impact on data security

Loss of EDP Department Control

The loss of EDP department control expresses a common personal and professional concern of many EDP managers. Some of this concern may be valid for the organization. Other reasons for this concern may relate more to a potential loss of status and power for the EDP manager. Consider the following factors that could contribute to the loss-of-control argument by your organization's EDP manager.

1. Loss of Power

Prior to the '60s, computers were used for important, but unglamorous work. They were good for processing payrolls and performing scientific calculations, but they were too expensive and too limited in capabilities to use for the work of other organization departments.

The introduction of faster, more reliable computers, with significantly increased on-line data storage capacity, during the '60s and '70s allowed data processing managers to capture control of organizations' data and processing resources. The power base of basic critical systems was then expanded to include other high-visibility financial applications such as billing, receivables, payables, and inventory systems.

Each of these systems could be easily justified as batch applications within a mix of other applications, which could then be used to collectively justify large central EDP departments. The result was the creation of an increasingly important EDP function that had to be courted for a priority of processing service.

The head of a large organization's EDP department during the '60s and early '70s was without rival. He held a mysterious management position and was responsible for a multimillion-dollar budget. A high degree of technical knowledge and a specialized vocabulary helped to keep away the uninitiated.

2. User Progression from Micros to Minis

The use of one small microcomputer in itself does not pose a substantial threat to a loss of control because a micro is limited in the amount of processing and printing that can be performed. However, it does provide the user with an opportunity to begin to learn what she can do independently of the data processing department. The direct result can be the addition of more microcomputers, or, with a modest investment of capital, progression to the use of a minicomputer.

A modest investment of capital, fifty- to one-hundred-thousand dollars, would allow a business department manager who was once at the mercy of the data processing department to purchase a large minicomputer. A minicomputer, the next step up from a microcomputer, isn't much larger than two or three filing cabinets, and can easily support the data processing requirements of a small company or a department within a larger company. Typically, they can be independently used to process payrolls, maintain an inventory, or handle receivables and billings.

Specialized vendors provide ready-to-use, "canned," software for minis that enable the business manager to become his own data processing manager without substantial, if any, need to rely on the data processing department. Spinoff minicomputer operations are truly a threat to the loss of control for the data processing manager.

3. Loss of Jurisdiction

It should be easy to determine the jurisdictional control of your organization's data processing manager. Simply find out, if you don't already know, if you can purchase any data processing equipment or services without the EDP manager's approval. The EDP manager is in control if she must approve your request for a microcomputer.

If your EDP manager currently has control of EDP expenditures, why should she realistically want to give any part of it up? You would not want to give up any comparable level of control.

Microcomputers are forcing the jurisdictional control issue to be opened in many organizations. Micros are sufficiently inexpensive to be purchased within the spending authority of many business managers who will either use them personally or obtain them for the use of their subordinates. The result has been the sudden appearance of micros in organizations without consultation, let alone the approval, of the EDP manager.

Some EDP managrs have accepted the demand for microcomputers as beneficial to the organization or perhaps an inevitability, and have provided purchasing advice, education, and company discount programs. Other EDP managers are fighting a losing battle to maintain control by asserting technical and jurisdictional reasons against micro purchases.

Impact on Organizational Data Systems

Microcomputers can have a very real impact on data systems that involve both the operations and the security of the organization.

A microcomputer can be made to look like a computer terminal to a larger computer application system. Operationally, this allows the user to collect and preprocess data prior to submitting it to the application system. The application system thinks that it is getting raw data.

The preprocessed data would seem like an advantage. The data is input by user personnel. This reduces that data processing department's budget. Input error rates can be reduced by actions taken at the entry point. The control concern is: "Who is checking what the micro, and its users, have done to the data without anyone else's knowledge?"

Microcomputers also impact the organization's data by providing the means for users to maintain and share large volumes of data independently without the central EDP or the EDP audit department's knowledge. The micro user may feel that this is both beneficial and expeditious. It is not desirable from a control perspective.

The technical capability to develop large microprocessor-based independent data systems that incorporate telecommunications networks is available. Unfortunately, these systems are easier to build than to control; especially when the systems are built to avoid the control and standardization requirements of the organization.

Impact on Data Security

The introduction of microcomputers into an organization's computer network can have a definite impact, especially if the data processing manager is not aware that it has happened. All that is required of the end user is to purchase a microcomputer that can emulate, or appear to a host computer, as a terminal.

At the most basic level, this would allow the user to copy and retain large volumes of the organization's data totally without management's knowledge. At a more advanced level, it would provide a tool for breaking the security systems of the unsuspecting host computer simply because a micro can rapidly and repetitively try more password combinations than a human terminal operator could perform.

It would be nice to think that your organization's professionally run computer has been protected against an internal microcomputer assault. However, it may not have been adequately secured because the replacement of terminals with microcomputers is against company policy, and data processing management is unaware that it is happening.

Microcomputer attachment to a host computer has yet another advantage that can be a security liability. They can create a dialup telecommunications entry to the main computer where none previously existed. All that is required is to equip the micro with the proper inexpensive communications devices and the micro user can open the host computer to the world.

The impact of microcomputers and microcomputer security will clearly continue. Expect to find security reference material in this area being published prolifically. An excellent current reference is the "SECURITY OF PERSONAL COMPUTER SYSTEMS: A Management Guide" which was prepared by the National Bureau of Standards. (NBS Special Publication 500-120.)

chapter 13

Keeping Up with Changing Security Requirements

This chapter summarizes the key issues that are discussed in this handbook. It provides a perspective on what to do to take advantage of security opportunities to stay ahead of security problems.

Keeping your security program current requires the awareness, understanding and support of every employee in the organization. From the chief executive officer who issues policies and directs that resources be made available, down the chain of command to the lowest level employee who has access to data and processing resources, each member of the organization must actively participate in the protection of the organization's resources.

Here, in summarizing the key issues discussed in this handbook, are fourteen specific suggestions to help you to keep your security program current.

1. Know who's on first.

Security is a management responsibility, not a technician's problem. Identify which managers have specific security responsibilities and hold them accountable for making cost-effective decisions to control the assets for which they are responsible.

2. Periodically review all policies, standards, and procedures.

An organization's policies, standards, and procedures are the most important means to advise all employees what management expects of them. The policies, standards, and procedures must be current with respect to what is to be accomplished, the manner in which it is to be achieved, and what may be expected if compliance is not maintained.

Build a realistic requirement for compliance with security policies, standards, and procedures into job descriptions and the employee performance appraisal process. Get the message across that "security is everybody's business."

3. Be practical with security.

Security programs have a very practical benefit. They reduce losses and the potential for embarrassment. However, they will be viewed as a impediment to productivity and a burden by some employees and customers. Balance the cost of every control with the benefit of the control. Also, be people oriented; find control solutions that will work in the environment into which they are placed.

4. Be certain that you have a workable DCRP.

Don't accept the presence of a "fat book" as the equivalent of a disaster contingency recovery plan. A plan doesn't exist if it is not maintained and tested regularly.

Periodically review the critical and discretionary application systems that the plan addresses. The systems and their recovery requirements can be expected to change as the needs of the business change, and as the applications themselves are changed.

Keep the components of the plan (data files, programs, procedures, documentation, inventories, contact lists, and the like) current between tests. Have your staff, as well as the EDP audit department, review them on a scheduled basis.

Test the plan on a schedule that meets the needs of the business units that are protected by the plan. Include unannounced tests as a supplement to the scheduled testing program.

5. Periodically review the effectiveness of your computer security program.

Keep your computer program current by regularly reviewing it. Use qualitative and/or quantitative risk analysis techniques to identify and substantiate the cost-effectiveness of controls that are in effect, and those that are being considered for implementation.

6. Emphasize individual accountability.

Employee accountability will be critical to the success of the organization's security program. Management, in addition to clearly defining what it expects of each employee, must develop systems that detect irregularities, and follow up to ensure that the goals and objectives of the organization are achieved in an honest and thorough manner.

7. Periodically review the effectiveness of data access control systems.

Expect changing technology to continue to change your data access control system requirements. Periodically reevaluate the effectiveness of the logical access control systems that you are using, and compare any unmet requirements with new product offerings. Additionally, you may need to implement data encryption products to supplement the abilities of access control systems, to ensure that data which is stored and communicated is protected from modification and disclosure.

8. Periodically review all application systems for obsolescence.

Computer application systems have a life cycle that is dependent on what the application must accomplish and the technology that is being used to meet its objectives. Replace those systems that are no longer cost-effective to maintain, or that will soon become technologically obsolete.

9. Beat the auditors to the punch.

Don't wait for the audit department to find security and control deficiencies. Train your staff to build systems that are secure. Encourage your staff to identify and remedy security and productivity problems as part of daily operations and system maintenance activities.

10. Keep current with legislative and regulatory changes.

Public and governmental concern with computer-related fraud and abuse, personal privacy, and unethical corporate conduct will continue to be a driving factor for legislative and regulatory changes. The direct result of these changes will be more stringent control and security requirements that will impact:

- what information may be collected
- how and to whom information may be disseminated
- how the accuracy, completeness, and timeliness of information is ensured
- the demonstrable adequacy of security measures that protect information and information processing resources
- the demonstrable adequacy of disruption and disaster recovery contingency plans

11. Plan for increased physical access control.

Physical access control will grow in importance as microcomputers become common throughout the organization. The micros and the data that they process will require increasingly more protection at a level that is consistent with the sensitivity of the applications that they support.

12. Pay particular attention to microcomputers.

Microcomputers will continue to dramatically change the way information is processed. Almost any employee can create a mini-data center without the knowledge of security or audit management. The direct result of this can be processing without standards, controls or adequate backup. Immediate and continuing management attention is needed to gain and maintain a level of control that will ensure that the micros are used in a manner consistent with the overall security policies of the organization.

Additionally, it is important to understand that the use of microcomputers by people other than employees (customers, vendors, hackers, and so forth) will continue to impact the organization's overall data security program. Microcomputer security implications must be stressed as part of the organization's continuing risk analysis program.

13. Don't accept computer-related abuse.

Hackers and authorized employees who invade your computer systems and damage or steal your assets (money, data, and processing resources) pose a very serious potential threat to your organization. Aggressively discipline and/or prosecute every detected computer abuser.

14. Provide the means for employees to recommend improvements and to report security violations.

Management must both encourage employees to actively support the organization's security program and provide the means for employee recommendations to receive appropriate recognition. Get the message across that all suggestions will be welcomed and will be reviewed by management; that those suggestions that could result in cost-effective improvements will be implemented; that those suggestions that are not implemented will receive an explanation as to why they were not accepted.

Provide the means to receive and act upon complaints and reports of security violations without recrimination to the complainant.

Index